MANAGI
TO SUCCEED

MANAGING TO SUCCEED

My Life in Football Management

HOWARD WILKINSON
with DAVID WALKER

MAINSTREAM
PUBLISHING

EDINBURGH AND LONDON

To all my family.
Thanks for your tolerance.

First published in Great Britain in 1992 by
MAINSTREAM PUBLISHING COMPANY (EDINBURGH) LTD
7 Albany Street
Edinburgh EH1 3UG

ISBN 1 85158 499 4

A catalogue record for this book is available from the British Library

Typeset in 12/14pt Garamond by Blackpool Typesetting Services Ltd,
Blackpool
Printed in Great Britain by Butler and Tanner Ltd, Frome, Somerset

CONTENTS

Chapter 1

HAIL THE CONQUERING HEROES

'The months of hard work, tactical drills, analysis of opponents only paid off because the Leeds players showed the most magnificent collective attitude and pulled together remorselessly.'

Winning is an obsession in professional football and that's why there are just two types of manager. There are those who have been sacked already and those who will be sacked in the future. The stark reality of our chosen profession inevitably sharpens the wits and makes a manager savour the precious moments of glory when his team accomplish tangible success.

I remember seeing George Graham leap from the dug-out at Liverpool on that memorable Friday night when Arsenal achieved the 2-0 victory over their closest rivals to clinch the 1989 Championship. I also recall Don Howe's ecstatic reaction in celebration when the great Arsenal double-winning side of 1971 secured their title. I envied the feelings both men had experienced at the moment the Championship was won and the knowledge, deep in their consciousness, that they had achieved the ultimate goal of all managers and coaches in this country.

In the immediate aftermath of Leeds United's Championship triumph last April I was dumbfounded. There I was, sat in silence in the dining-room at my home with a plate of roast lamb and a glass of red wine in front of me, while the people in the lounge were dancing, laughing and celebrating. I conducted a thankfully brief television interview via the telephone after our arch-rivals Manchester United had lost at Liverpool, a result that ensured we could not be overtaken. I admit, on that occasion, words failed me.

Friends have subsequently teased me that I was intoxicated by something more potent and more easily bottled than success, but the truth is that the sheer enormity of being involved in the re-birth of a once great club and Leeds' coronation as the best team in England left me totally stunned. I have never experienced anything like it. I was speechless.

I had maintained all along that the race for the title would go to the final week. Perhaps I had prepared myself for that scenario too well. When we were crowned a week early I found it difficult to comprehend the impact of that result at Anfield. I must admit my five-year-old son Ben had been regaling the diners at my home with details of United's downfall on Merseyside. At 2-0, with only minutes remaining, the outcome was inevitable. Yet such was my state of mind that I was still telling myself we might have to wait another seven days.

Instead of watching the game live from Liverpool I enjoyed a late Sunday lunch with my wife Sam, assistant-manager Michael Hennigan and his wife Sonia, along with managing-director Bill Fotherby and his wife Josie. My eldest son Damian was supposed to be with us but when he found out about the television embargo he decided to stay away. Once the day of glory was assured he quickly turned up and the champagne began to flow freely as we were joined by media people.

The day was so momentous and yet I still find it easier to recall my precise feelings from, say, 12 months earlier than to detail my emotions of Sunday, 26 April 1992.

There was a great sense of relief when I finally accepted the notion that I was the manager of the new League champions – and also a sense of sadness. In a strange way I felt a tinge of regret in the belief that what was happening with Leeds might have happened with Sheffield Wednesday if things had gone differently there, but I'll enlarge on that later. At Leeds we had achieved a footballing miracle, given even greater stature by the time-scale we were aiming to work within when I took control at Elland Road three and a half years earlier. I did become emotional and tears were shed. Despite all the odds I had fulfilled an ambition that had been with me ever since that day, some 20 years earlier, when I decided to risk all and opt for an eventful career in management.

Guiding a club to the summit of the English game and into the European Cup has always been my ambition since those far-off days in my mid-twenties when I realised that I was gaining no sense of fulfilment from being a Third Division footballer with Brighton. I wanted to make a career as either a football coach or manager. I had tasted life as a player but sometimes in life you have to take the opportunity to do what you believe you're good at and I realised one of my assets was passing on knowledge to others, be it as a school teacher after I had qualified from Sheffield University, or in my formative years as player-manager at Boston United of the Northern Premier League. In fact, there were lessons gleaned from those unfashionable days that were assiduously applied during Leeds' title-winning campaign.

Boston won their Championship three times while I was with them. You had to possess a special kind of commitment to the footballing cause in those non-League days. You had to work in civvy street and then have the interest and desire to fulfil your ambitions in football. It was a case of constant self-analysis. Those that couldn't maintain the passion fell by the wayside. There were others, like Jim Smith, Ron Atkinson and David Pleat, who honed their managerial talents in that pool before jumping out to swim with the big fish.

Bill Shankly, the legendary Liverpool manager, once pointed out that a successful club was built around players of great durability. For a shrewd manager, looking around your dressing-room and seeing players with steely determination and genuine strength of character is a critical matter. The slightest chink in a player's emotional and competitive make-up can be exposed at the most vital moment for your club. And that's why, when I analyse now the makings of a Championship team at Elland Road, I recognise the strength of character that was needed to see us through those final, testing days of an exhausting season.

Team spirit is never easy to develop. A team willing to accept the work ethic as a fundamental principle and then nurture collective aspirations is ideal. Conversely, life becomes much harder when you have to cope with players who care predominantly for their own aspirations and the opportunity to display their individual talents as the first and foremost precepts of their careers. The Leeds players proved they could display their talents but, most pleasingly, showed a growing awareness that talent on its own was not enough.

The progress we've made at Elland Road has to be viewed over a three-year period. You must consider the achievement of winning the Second Division title in 1990 and then following that up by finishing fourth on our return to the First Division. Running parallel to the League form was a League Cup semi-final appearance against Manchester United and the fact that in the FA Cup, the Champions-elect, Arsenal, were forced to face four breathtaking ties against us before defeating us by the odd goal in three. The resilience within the team was visible for all to see.

To go on from that intial platform to win the title must rank as the most telling testimony to a team's character there has ever been. All along the players accepted that they were not part of the biggest squad in the League. But they believed me when I told them that we could field the best team and that if we were to win the Championship we would have to dig deeper into our reserves than any team had done in the past. The months of hard work, tactical drills, analysis of opponents only paid off because those Leeds players showed the most magnificent collective attitude and pulled together remorselessly.

After almost eight months, and including cup defeats against out major adversaries from Old Trafford, the Leeds lads had shown the backbone to see the job through and ulti- mately seize the Championship. After an 18-year gap we were hailed as the country's finest, yet, just 22 days earlier, we had suffered a humiliating 4-0 defeat at Manchester City that saw most critics write off our title chances and place the Championship crown firmly on Alex Ferguson's team.

I was privileged to witness individual players respond in the most marvellous way to that set-back at Maine Road. If they hadn't there was a danger our season might peter out and provoke a mood of bitter anti-climax to engulf Elland Road because on that sunny day in Manchester the best thing we had going for us was the noisy and unstinting support of our massive travelling army of fans, the troop who call themselves Sergeant Wilko's Barmy Army. Sadly, the team did not match their passion. I sat down and analysed individual aspects of that defeat as well as the collective team performance. I came to conclusions that I believe proved to be vital ingredients in what happened over the next three weeks.

Inevitably, I faced calls to make wholesale changes to the team, to punish the players who had not been up to scratch against the Mancunians. I decided the right approach to the run-in was to go back to our most experienced, proven team. Instead of chopping and changing I chose to back the players who had performed so creditably for the previous six months and leave them to win or lose the title. In my wisdom I felt it was better to return to the pattern and team play we had developed through an informative pre-season period rather than to clutch at straws and pray for one-off football miracles. There was one high-profile victim though.

That selection policy resulted in demotion to the rank of substitute for the man who had become a cult figure among the Leeds fans after just two months on loan with us – French striker Eric Cantona. I knew the crowd wanted to see him in action but I recognised Eric would have to be deployed in a sensible, tactical manner to help him adapt to life in England. From now on his limited, but crucial, role would be that of a substitute. His virtuosity and flair would flower better in the last 30 minutes of matches when opponents had lost some of their bite. Like David Fairclough in Bob Paisley's Liverpool team, Eric would become our 'supersub'.

Playing in a fast, physical game, such as the one at Maine Road, was very different to anything Eric had encountered on his travels with Marseille and Nimes. And Eric knew it. I was also reminded of the situation at Manchester City, some 20 years earlier, when Malcolm Allison, to his and the club's loss, persisted in playing new signing Rodney Marsh. City blew their title chances. I called the players together for a meeting during the following week and explained my thoughts for the climax to the season. Eric sat there impassively, so afterwards I spoke to him privately in my best French to make sure he understood. I realised he might not like the news but it had to be done. I subsequently learned that he was somewhat shocked and disappointed but he never failed to give of his best when he was called on. It went better than I could have hoped. As a substitute he did play a significant role over the next few weeks, coping much better when thrown into the fray after the pace had slowed down in the second half.

Given Eric's reputation as 'Le Brat' some people will be surprised by the references I received from France when I enquired about Eric's personality. Michel Platini, at the time

France's national team manager, and his assistant Gerard Houillier, spoke in terms of Eric's 'sense of justice', 'intelligence' and 'loyalty'. They also admitted he could be 'impulsive' but enthused about his natural skill level. Cantona's recruitment was a major gamble on my part. A gamble I had to take following the broken wrist sustained by Lee Chapman in the FA Cup third round defeat against United.

Once we had faced up to the nightmare probability of losing our most reliable marksman for at least six weeks I knew it was vital that I appear calm and in control of the situation. Deep down I was quaking with nerves about it but I announced my intention to try young Gary Speed as a stop-gap. Despite all the suggestions in the past, especially from managing-director Fotherby, that we had no adequate cover for Chapman and might pay for it, we were now facing that precise reality. Gary can head the ball well, he has good touch as a target man and probably offered greater skills than Chapman but the one thing he lacked was Chappy's desire to score goals of all types in every game. Chappy has that priceless instinct for turning up in the right place at the right time and is so single-minded you sometimes sense his own goal-scoring record is more important to him than anything else in the game.

It was also critical that the confidence level among the crowd was not affected by Chapman's absence so when Cantona failed to agree terms with Sheffield Wednesday following a week's trial at Hillsborough I sensed the time had come for dramatic action. It was England assistant-manager Lawrie McMenemy who put me on the Cantona trail. He telephoned me after meeting Platini at an international game. I understand Wednesday asked Eric to spend a second week on trial but he was not happy with this idea. Before he could check out of his Sheffield hotel and fly home I arrived to whisk him up the motorway to Leeds.

I wasn't in Trevor Francis's position at Hillsborough with a surplus of strikers. The chance to examine one who a few months earlier had announced his premature retirement in France was worth the risk. I had to take a gamble. We agreed a deal to take Eric on an immediate three-month loan with a view to a permanent transfer. Nimes, his French club, would receive £100,000 in lieu of his services and we paid his wages but I reasoned that at that price he would prove an absolute bargain if he could help us qualify for Europe.

During his first training session you could see the benefits of having Cantona around. His instinctive vision and passing skills were exquisite. I think we both knew he was being scrutinised by some very worldly wise Leeds players who would be able to spot any flaws or glamorous trick shots performed more for effect than victory. Eric lifted the proceedings to a higher level with a series of devastating flicks and passes. You could see the other players quickly develop a high regard for his talent. Would that high regard also apply to his character?

In terms of Cantona's learning process in England, the Maine Road experience should not be regarded as a total disaster. I knew he had to be pulled out of the starting line-up in future but my selection policy did not affect the astonishing response he generated from the crowd. The bond was inexplicable. The Leeds fans worshipped the swarthy Frenchman's every move and he was appreciative of their warm welcome. He attracted more media coverage than any player I've every signed, including Gordon Strachan. Journalists arrived from all over Europe to meet him and he was not just contributing to sports articles either. He gave interviews on art, philosophy and politics. A natural room-mate for David Batty, I thought immediately.

By the end of the season I felt he deserved the chance to stay at Elland Road on a permanent deal. In fact, at a fee of around £900,000 he could prove a real bargain because that is the sort of price put on the heads of lower division strikers these days once a club of Leeds' stature show any interest. I'm also grateful that he does not collect cautions with the same abandon that he attracts parking tickets. Eric seems to think yellow lines represent some eccentric British road decoration.

We faced five more matches in the run-in after the defeat against City. We were never beaten and won four of them, the two goals we conceded in that bizarre 3-2 victory at Sheffield United being the only goals against us following the Maine Road massacre. Again, when we could only get a goal-less draw at Liverpool with three matches remaining, predictions of a title near-miss abounded. We confounded our critics.

I firmly believe that for football success it is far more important to have character than to be a character. When people talk about characters they are generally referring to fringe events, like who can pull off the daftest dressing-room pranks and who is the master of wit and repartee. Professional football, just like any sport at the highest level, is about truth. It is out on that pitch, in front of thousands of witnesses, that players find out about themselves – and about their colleagues. Frank Lloyd Wright, the famous American architect, once claimed, 'The physician can bury his mistakes, but the architect can only advise his client to plant vines.' Players can feign injury, publicly blame outside influences or the team's tactics in an attempt to camouflage their failings but, inevitably, the weak are found out. An unhappy player may demand a transfer and bolt to pastures new for a fresh start but the seeds of doubt and failure have already been planted. Conversely, if a footballer treats his sport with honesty and respect he will encounter the truth – and be better for it.

The First Division is a graveyard for self-satisfaction. Football is a dreamworld and for the spectators' sake you have to take note of the escapist fantasy the game can offer them. But, at this level, you have to win. In the lower divisions you can occasionally find a chairman with realistic aspirations for his club and the view that what matters most is entertainment. Clubs like Leeds, Liverpool, Arsenal and Manchester United must pursue glory – nothing less will do. Those demands are then passed on to the playing-staff. As manager you attempt to protect your charges but there is no known antidote to the pain of failure at a club like Leeds, just as nobody will ever be able to take away the radiant glow of success when the dreams of many millions are fulfilled.

Nobody could have asked more at Leeds from young players like Speed and David Batty during that titanic spring of 1992. They could have hidden behind the innocence and inexperience of youth and seen the testing events as another interesting lesson in their football development, safe in the belief that nobody would blame them for any potential failure. Ironically, during my initial three and a half years in charge at Leeds, I constantly stressed the gospel that only through accepting responsibility would either of the duo blossom into the great players their rich talents deserved. Thankfully, when we needed them, they came good.

Batty is a player of far greater natural ability than he displayed in his formative years. He does undoubtedly possess the tenacity of a terrier but when you scrutinise him on a daily basis in training you realise the burgeoning talent bubbling away inside the aggressive shell. He somehow went three years between scoring his first and second League goals. He knows that kind of drought is not good enough for a midfielder with England international aspirations, yet his technique at volleys and half-volleys and in passing the ball long and short is impressive. I did begin to wonder if the indignity of missing chances was not hurting David enough or, then again, maybe the embarrassment of his miss was the real deterrent for the future.

Batty will rightly replay to his grandchildren in years to come the video recording of his marvellous solo goal against Notts County when he sprinted 50 yards downfield before lashing an unstoppable shot into the top corner. It was the sort of televised goal careers have been built on, good enough to clinch a lucrative transfer to foreign shores. I was happy to remind him that what the coaching staff see him do in training was now being repeated in public.

I would cite Speed as our outstanding individual performer over the season. Perhaps the greatest tribute I could pay him was to recall the way, in times of adversity, I could ask Gary to fill virtually any position in the team. He had come to prominence as a wide left-midfielder yet we know inside the club that he has the vision and passing ability to operate in a central role.

Speed's ability in the air is a major asset and I doubt whether, inch for inch, there are many better headers of the ball in the country. That aerial strength has seen Arsenal switch David O'Leary to right-back to combat the way Speed has out-jumped England international right-back Lee Dixon. But those are the areas of the field people have expected Gary to perform in and, to a lesser extent, there was no great surprise when he has moved in an emergency to left-back.

In Chapman's absence though he produced some creditable displays at centre-forward and then, in his biggest personal test, he filled in as a stop-gap right-back following Mel Sterland's ankle injury. He may not have found that the easiest role to relate to but adapt he did – and without any complaint. Obviously, given our clubs' immense rivalry, I'm abundantly aware of the talent of Manchester United's attacking prodigy, Ryan Giggs. He is a tremendous prospect and won the players' union award as the best young player last season. Overall though, I believe that award should have gone to another Welshman, Speed of Leeds, and perhaps it would if the PFA had made their nominations at the end of the season instead of at the mid-term point.

There were so many on-field heroes who played significant parts in our pursuit of England's most prestigious trophy. I recall in those final games the way that John Lukic rose to the challenge of creating his own little piece of history as a goalkeeper who had won League Championship medals with two teams – Arsenal and Leeds. He endured a nightmare in that heavy defeat at Maine Road yet when we needed a superlative display from him at Anfield in our next away game he responded in the most magnificent fashion.

There were times when I used to willingly bang the 'Lukic for England' drum but given Graham Taylor's reluctance to select the big fellow that particular message began to sound hollow. It shouldn't have though. Since he re-joined us in a £1 million transfer from Arsenal, John has produced some superb displays and kept us alive in matches that could easily have swung against us. If you sit down at the end of the season and analyse your results you can quickly quantify just how many points a good goalie has earned your team. Lukic has been vital.

There was also an unfortunate irony in having paid that much money for a keeper Leeds discovered as a schoolboy only to release for just £75,000 to Arsenal in 1983. When we were searching for a potential goalkeeper signing it seemed that virtually every player we looked at had an Elland Road connection. John was the obvious one and his replacement at Highbury, David Seaman, had also been signed, groomed and sold for just £5,000 to Peterborough.

In front of Lukic, centre-backs Chris Whyte and Chris Fairclough were so often unsung and underrated yet they stood firm to play their part in what we knew would be a momentous climax. I did not see a better centre-back than Whyte last season. I'm still amazed at his lack of recognition. He missed just one game and has to rate as one of the best buys I've ever had the good fortune to make. Against Liverpool I asked Fairclough to man-mark John Barnes, who had endured a miserable, injury-wracked season. Despite all his problems though, I still felt Barnes was the most gifted attacking player in England, a status he emphasised in creating match-winning goals in the FA Cup semi-final and the vital League game against Manchester United. While Barnes may not have possessed the zest to launch his stunning, individual sorties he still had the passing vision and touch to unhinge any defence. It was Fairclough's task to stop him.

Chris was so good that day that a defender groomed in the wiles of the Italian League could not have bettered him. He was ruthlessly single-minded, studiously attentive to his task and quite brilliant at seeing the job through. When you see an opposition forward seizing a bouncing ball and setting his sights to shoot, you relax if Fairclough is the defender racing to shut him down. Chris is so brave he will not flinch from physical contact or confrontations. He is also scrupulously fair and fulfils the maxim of a good defender by playing hard but within the rules.

The one real personal set-back for Chris in a fine season was his dismissal against Everton a few weeks after we had hit top spot in the First Division. I felt sorry for Chris because he became the innocent victim that weekend of a concerted Press campaign to clear his name and bring about the advent of video evidence as a means of defence at Football Association disciplinary hearings.

Fairclough was sent off after a flare-up with Everton midfielder Mark Ward. Chris undoubtedly fouled Ward as Everton attempted to clear their lines at a Leeds corner-kick but, as he lay on the pitch, Ward appeared to have a kick at Chris and, as he attempted to jump to his feet to carry on the dispute, Fairclough pushed him with the flat of his palm and walked away. Referee Tony Ward allowed Ward to escape but Fairclough was shown the red card. Afterwards, the referee told a respected journalist from *The Independent* newspaper that the Leeds player had been sent off for violent conduct, namely kicking an opponent.

Fairclough was understandably upset at this because the video evidence proved he had never attempted to kick Ward. The referee was wrong. To be fair, virtually every journalist present at the match made mention of the injustice and the fact that by studying the replay the referee would have to accept his mistake. Chris even admitted, 'The only thing I did was push Wardy back down when he threatened to get busy and make something more of the situation.'

The outcome was predictable. By the time the referee's report arrived at Lancaster Gate two extra words appertaining to the incident had been introduced. The referee asserted that Fairclough was sent off 'for violent conduct – kicking and striking an opponent'. It may have been with the flat of his hand that he palmed Ward downwards but, in official circles, he had struck an opponent. For his sins he received an automatic three-match suspension.

Our start to the season had been a total anti-climax. Pre-season is a physically demanding time and much of the motivation to inspire players through the early workload is the anticipation of the first game. A football season is a long haul and by the end of it you need three months to recover. But when the players return for pre-season work you can see them straining at the leash to get into the frame again. Given this upsurge in expectations, imagine the disappointment that deflates everyone when you're told a few days before the off that your first game has been postponed. Unfortunately, we couldn't play at Selhurst Park on the opening Saturday because the work on the stadium detailed by Crystal Palace had not been completed on time.

We were all bitterly disappointed. Our build-up work had been so good. There had been no serious injuries. Everyone looked fit and well and I remember being particularly excited with the little bits and pieces we had seen from new-boy Rod Wallace in training. Rod had joined us with his twin brother Ray in a joint £1.7 million transfer from Southampton. I had been looking for someone who might carve something out of nothing when we were under pressure, perhaps away from Elland Road. Rod looked the part with his pace and ability to go past opponents.

I remember thinking strength could be a problem for Rod. We would have to work on that over the next three of four years. Rod needed to be able to sustain his effort level, not only throughout a game, but also throughout a season. I took him on one side in the early stages and explained this to him. Our agreed target was for Rod to produce 32 good performances in a minimum of 36 appearances.

Our second major summer signing was left-back Tony Dorigo from Chelsea. Tony returned from England's summer tour to Australia and the Far East with a hernia problem, which didn't go down too well. We were assured by the surgeon, though, that the normal six weeks' recuperation would be sufficient and it must be said Tony did brilliantly. He was back in record time and after four weeks turned out in a friendly match against Shelbourne of Dublin. The Shelbourne game was part of a tour of Ireland involving another outing in Dublin and a trip down to Cork. I like visiting our friends at Shelbourne. In fact, a trip to Dublin has become something of a pilgrimage for Leeds. It all started soon after I took over at Elland Road and, it must be said, the Irish don't seem to tire of us visiting them. We have a terrific following over there and can certainly pack the crowds in.

It was in these pleasant surroundings that Tony settled himself into the team. It was an impressive sight which epitomised his approach to his profession. He bases his game on brain-power rather than brawn. He was neat, tidy and greyhound-quick. In many respects you don't know you've got him around the place really. I think it was my assistant Michael Hennigan who claimed, 'Tony must be the only posh Aussie in existence.'

We had signed two youngsters from Sheffield Wednesday in Jon Newsome and David Weatherall. Both were seen very much as buys for the future, although big Jon came into his own at a very demanding juncture last season. David had a year left at Sheffield University and I was prepared for him to 'waste' that year in a football sense. Even so, he made it to the substitutes' bench for a run of five games and his undoubted promise was evident for all to see.

Within a couple of weeks of joining us in pre-season training Jon got the backroom staff a little excited. There were signs that he might just flower a little sooner than any of us had predicted. Disappointment was just around the corner though, when he developed a knee problem. It was spring before we could even think about Jon again.

After a few failed attempts in the past I finally signed Steve Hodge from Nottingham Forest in time for our assault on the Championship. I'd had to wait through the summer though because, like Dorigo, he had been away on the England tour. I thought then, and I maintain now, that on his day Hodgey is one of the best midfield players in the country. When I signed him I told him that he should be playing for his country regularly and after watching the European Championships in Sweden I'm even more convinced. When you itemise the characteristics required in a top-quality midfielder you realise Steve possesses the lot. The late Don Revie always maintained that the ideal midfield man should be able to pass, tackle and run and score goals. Many players have earned themselves lofty reputations by doing just two of those things. Hodgey can do the lot. In fact, when you analyse his goal-scoring ratio in recent years he does that job from midfield better than anyone around.

During our pre-transfer talks I emphasised that I wanted Leeds to have the best midfield team in the country in Batty, McAllister, Speed, Strachan and Hodge. Sadly, last season, as far as Steve as an individual was concerned, was a disappointment. In fact, it was disappointing for him . . . and me. We knew during his last year at Forest he had suffered a run of injuries which unfortunately continued at Leeds. There were times when I'm sure England manager Graham Taylor, Brian Clough and I felt we were banging our extremely big heads against a brick wall. By the end of the season, and amid a sea of frustration, surgery finally revealed and cured Steve's big problem. He had been carrying a calf muscle injury for a long time. I still believe Hodge is as good as any midfielder around. The big challenge now is for Steve to convince himself of that fact. He must put the last couple of years behind him.

I'm always open to new ideas, new philosophies and research which might, in some way or other, help the players in my team win football matches. When I was a player at Brighton, under manager Archie Macauley's guidance, we had some remarkable preparations for important matches and cup-ties. There were liberal doses of sherry and raw eggs, calves' foot jelly, fillet steak and plenty of walks on the sea front where we were taken to fill our lungs with the ozone. I'd like to think that the experience and research gleaned from science and technology have taken our sports medicine a little further. But there are still times when footballers underwhelm you with the desire to search for the truth. Keeping up the search for what you think is good, while discarding the rest, is not easy these days. It just took football a long time to wake up to the fact that it was part of the sports science world and not a separate planet spinning around in its own universe. Now it has stirred from its slumbers and, I must admit, in certain respects, I wonder if we're better for it?

Football can have more akin with a bus than the sleek sports coupé we'd like it to be. Like a bus it can carry a lot of passengers. I could spend every day of my working life sitting in meetings with psychologists, hypnotherapists, fitness experts, dieticians, sports scientists and technologists. All write tremendous letters to me, totally convinced that they have discovered the secret to sport's 'Holy Grail', the perpetual route to victory. The pity is that among this throng there are genuine people with a genuine commitment who are keen to further our understanding and knowledge. Unfortunately, sorting out the wheat from the chaff is nigh impossible because of the vast amounts of experts fighting for places on the bus.

I'm also afraid too many of the experts have seen soccer as

the golden goose. The goose, though, only lays her golden eggs with extreme reluctance and I have found the big draw-back with certain experts is that they are good at analysing a problem and suggesting possible solutions but there are few who will provide a blueprint before you encounter your crises.

A manager, out of necessity, faces familiar criteria each season. You can try to present your ideas to the players a little differently, emphasise your determination to bring out the best in the group you're working with and, critically, insist on a desire from the staff that they want to be better footballers. Inevitably, sooner or later, such homespun logic as hard graft, sweat and concentration enter the equation. These are just as crucial for the players as they attempt to better themselves. There are still players, and managers for that matter, who believe that training is something to do between matches which makes the time go by more quickly. Entertainment, and not enlightenment, is the name of the game. As I've occasionally been known to utter in training, 'If it's entertainment you want, go to Butlin's for a fortnight and while you're away I'll buy a red coat.'

At the start of a new season there are three simple objec-tives I love to achieve as quickly as possible. I look for the first goal, the first point and the first victory. Clinch the hat-trick in your first game, as we did last season, and you're flying. Gary McAllister's goal came from David Batty's long throw to launch the campaign with a 1-0 victory over Nottingham Forest. It had been a good, all-round Leeds performance and while the narrow margin may have been misleading, I sometimes believe a tight victory like this can keep players on their toes more than if they become over-confident following a three or four-goal victory.

Our aim was simply to improve on finishing fourth in the previous season. If we could do that we would qualify for Europe, which was a major attraction. Everyone involved at Leeds would be delighted. We had the same nucleus of players but the additions should have improved our overall strength. However, playing assets are not the be-all and end-all. In the long term, team performance and results are inextricably linked. Basically, our task was to stick to the things we did well . . . but do them better.

My assessment of our rivals was that I did not see any team making such massive improvements that they would overshadow anything we could produce. As I told the players, 'Get around 84 points this season and you'll be unlucky if you're not the Champions.' I believe working on a two-points-per-game target was realistic for us. The theory still needed putting into operation. We had to concede as few goals as possible but definitely not at the expense of our own scoring ratio. We stuck by the old tried and trusted method of looking at blocks of ten games in isolation and reviewing the season at Christmas.

As it turned out, the planning looked like collapsing by October. Manchester United had made a storming start. I went to see them in their second game at Aston Villa where they won 1-0. They looked extremely tight. I remember commenting afterwards that if United scored just one goal against most teams they would win. If life in the Football League teaches you one thing it is that mental toughness is essential. It may not be in the best interests of quality football but the League is not designed to cater for the demands of the aesthete. You learn at the top that while the tempo of games increases after Christmas, the pace at which the points arrive can decrease considerably. My philosophy is quite simply, 'Perform, persist and the points will come. If you do your best and are beaten, have no regrets. Play through the season, reflect through the summer. Enjoy the triumphs and regret the defeats in May and June.'

The first manager to hail us potential Champions was Southampton's Ian Branfoot after we had won 4-1 at the Dell. It was a display that augured well for the future. Rod Wallace, back on his old stamping ground, produced precisely the sort

of performance that I'd be asking of him. And, despite
the scoreline, Southampton gave us a severe test. I remember
remarking afterwards that I was relieved to meet them early
in the season rather than later. A lot of preparation had
gone into what they were trying to do but it required time
to perfect. Gary Speed scored two great goals and really
looked the part while he was aided by Wallace's pace and
directness. I've known Ian Branfoot nearly 30 years, and
he's always been a confident fellow. But when he described
us as future League Champions I wondered if he was
seriously backing his good judgment or merely suffering from
shell-shock.

Success in cup football is always tangible. You know the
goal, the game, the result that makes your dreams come true
or leaves you waiting for another season to fulfil those ambitions of walking out at Wembley. In the League, though, you
never know which is the point that will win you the title or
the defeat that will get you relegated. I find the progression
of a season fascinating to observe and be part of. Our trip to
Manchester United was one of those games that, in retrospect, tell you an awful lot about your players and, it must be
stressed, a certain David was at his Batty best.

The stadium was full. The atmosphere matched the tem-
perature, which was boiling hot. An early Lee Chapman goal
from Speed's deep cross gave us a great start as we matched
United pass for pass, challenge for challenge. In the thick of
it was Batty who displayed no sign of nerves. His apparent
lack of respect for the game can sometimes be disturbing. At
twenty past two, with the tension mounting in the dressing-
room, he'll be prowling around, annoying everybody – but
that's Batts. He has an ice-cold temperament for even the
biggest of matches. I've spoken to him about his approach
and explained what suits him might not suit the rest of the
players. He has responded and finished up being made
captain when Gordon Strachan was absent, which is no
mean achievement.

I asked David before our game at Norwich whether he fancied the job of being stand-in skipper. He immediately jumped at the chance. I then went on to explain what the job entailed. I don't hand the armband to just anyone. It was an honour. Leeds were a special club with a famous reputation. We were going places and the captaincy was not just a case of carrying a ball out at the front of the line for kick-off and tossing a coin. He was stepping into the shoes of a skipper who had proved a major influence on the club's impressive progress. I told David he was a good player but not always a good professional. There is a big difference. Many aspects of playing football are instinctive. The game comes naturally to people like David, who makes decisions automatically – both physical and mental. But a good pro and a captain has to think differently. He has to weigh up what is good for others, not just himself. He has to see a bigger picture and show a great deal of respect for football, his team and the result.

He listened and didn't flinch, offer any excuses or any 'but gaffer, give me a break'. So the deed was done. In fact, I talked to the players as a group and repeated everything I had said to David. I know some of what I said raised the odd joke – all at Batty's expense – but he coped and dealt with the job in the right manner. He may have suffered a little embarrassment. Resentment? Not a bit of it.

During our match at Old Trafford, Batty was everywhere – tackling, heading, hustling, passing and generally setting the tempo of the game. The game was played on one of the hottest football days I've ever known in England and it was Bryan Robson who dragged United back into the frame. It was as if he was pulling the rest of the team along with him by sheer will-power. Robson snatched their late equaliser but Batty stood his ground and, as a result, so did the rest of the Leeds team. We came away with a well-earned point which within the progression of the League season might prove especially valuable.

There are certain matches, inevitably linked by traditional rivalry and a historical perspective, that transcend the level of normal competition and become events. There was very much a sense of occasion when Liverpool were the visitors to Elland Road. The memories of the old days when Don Revie's team were slugging it out at the top against Bill Shankly's Liverpool came pouring out. The newspapers were full of reminiscences from Billy Bremner, Jack Charlton, John Giles, Tommy Smith and Ron Yeats. Sadly, Liverpool's current manager Graeme Souness was not enjoying the best 12 months of his life and it was not the most cocksure Liverpool side to have departed from Merseyside that arrived wearing Liverpool's famous red shirts for this game. The previous April they had won 5-4 at Leeds and during the first half, when they raced into a four-goal lead, made us look like the bunch of young upstarts we probably were. On that day Liverpool knocked us back into the real world when we were perhaps beginning to think we were doing so admirably back in the top flight. They made sure we were aware of the First Division's order of supremacy.

Steve Hodge came into our side and produced a vintage performance this time. With two of his early tackles he set out his stall and our approach. As a result, the previous season's thrashing seemed to be forgotten. I had vowed after that heavy defeat never to play against Liverpool with a straightforward 4-4-2 formation, like the one they deploy so effectively. Batty was used as a forward sweeper and we managed to get at Liverpool straight away. Hodge took his goal in splendid fashion but we were also indebted to the defensive work of veteran John McClelland. In the first 20 minutes he was forced to turn and chase after both Dean Saunders and Ian Rush as they pursued through balls. On each occasion he outpaced them. At the ripe old age of 36 John was still one of the fastest men in football. As a senior professional his understanding of the game was immense and he had always done everything asked of him. He knew there would be times when I would ask him to step into the side in special circumstances or to cover an injury and he was always totally dependable. A little piece of history was made because our 1-0 victory was Leeds' first over Liverpool for 18 years.

Keeping success and failure in perspective is of paramount importance to a manager. I sensed this in a positive way when we achieved our next little milestone by defeating Oldham 1-0 on 26 October 1991 to climb to the top of the League for the first time in 17 years. We may have needed an own goal from Brian Kilcline – an old friend from our days together at Notts County – to clinch our victory over opponents who have traditionally caused Leeds numerous problems, but the surge of excitement among the fans reached tidal wave proportions. The scenes of celebration in and around Elland Road that day provided an insight into the kind of crowd reaction that would engulf the club later. Outwardly, I didn't attempt to pour too much cold water on the supporters' delight but I did feel the need to point out that their chants that we were already Champions were somewhat premature. Deep down I was so thrilled I wanted to jump over the stand. For yours truly it was the first time I had been top of the League during my 48 years! There was also the irony that our move to the top had been assisted by Manchester United's first defeat of the season at my old club, Sheffield Wednesday.

By the end of October, and with a third of our fixtures fulfilled, the First Division table read:

	P	W	D	L	F	A	Pts
1 Leeds Utd	14	8	5	1	25	12	29
2 Man Utd	13	8	4	1	21	7	28

After half a dozen games we had vowed in the dressing-room not to drop below second in the League. Now we had hit top spot and the poser was, should we contemplate still being there in May? In a word, 'no'. I decided the right way now would be to concentrate on performances and banish, as far as possible, from the minds of the players and the public thoughts of anything happening in the future. It was still so tight at the top. Inevitably, with two teams locked in combat like this, any minor slip would provide our rivals with the chance to climb above us into pole position. Within a week of ending that long wait we were held to a draw by Wimbledon at Selhurst Park while Manchester United defeated Sheffield United 2-0 to leap-frog back over us. The Wimbledon match was a drab, disappointing affair but I've left there empty-handed many times in the past. The point was more important than which team were League leaders for the opening of November.

It took Rod Wallace time to find the mark for Leeds though, and a strained hamstring, sustained when he was playing particularly well against Manchester City, didn't help his cause. But once he opened his League goal-scoring account for us against Queen's Park Rangers on 16 November there was no stopping him. He set off on the sort of purple patch Lee Chapman has made famous and found the target in four consecutive League games. Even more importantly, we won all four to move above the Manchester men again.

It was during this run of victories that we appeared in a televised game that I sense made many people aware of our progress. Aston Villa had been climbing up the First Division themselves under Ron Atkinson's management with Cyrille Regis enjoying an Indian summer working with his old managerial mentor, and Tony Daley displaying the pace and unpredictability that can make him such a difficult opponent to tie down.

We may not have won all our televised matches but I know from meeting the ITV and BBC executives that they were invariably delighted by the entertainment level and exciting crowd atmosphere generated at our games. That message was also conveyed by the BSkyB hierarchy after they clinched the latest television deal. We had our normal massive following at Villa Park for that Sunday game and ran out emphatic winners, 4-1. Technically, tactically, individually and collectively we were spot on that day. A great deal of importance was heaped on a tactical switch we made by handing the ever-reliable Chris Fairclough a man-marking job on Daley while utilising John McClelland at centre-back alongside Chris Whyte. Within this new defensive set-up Mel Sterland and Tony Dorigo were able to press forward more often and provide crosses for the strikers. Sterland had a hand in virtually everything and rounded off a superb display with a goal. His cross for Chapman's spectacular second was as good as you'll see anywhere in the world and showed, providing you give him enough of the ball, the contribution he can make. As a supply line at creating goals, Mel is second to none.

The influence of television coverage can not be underestimated. Victory in this match saw us discussed on a much wider stage as potential champions but the match when I felt we had shown we were on the right lines actually came at Villa Park 12 months earlier. A few days before our visit Villa had enjoyed a spectacular UEFA Cup victory over Inter Milan and were buoyant. On this occasion we man-marked Daley and handed the job to Chris Kamara, who diligently followed orders to snuff out the threat from the England winger. There were no cameras present to record our performance in a goalless draw but I was genuinely delighted by our display. We passed the ball sensibly and well. We showed we could keep possession against a good team. We didn't play simply for effect, there was purpose there. That Villa Park performance will stick in my mind for many years to come.

Nobody has yet managed to distil and retail that priceless gift called confidence but defeat is undoubtedly the best-known method of evaporating the precious sense of belief within a team. The odds against Leeds and Manchester United being paired against each other in both domestic cup competitions were evaluated at hundreds of thousands to one. The fact that our League meeting at Elland Road prefaced the cup-ties simply set the scene for a demanding, yet memorable, trilogy spanning just 17 days. My biggest worry was that with the rigours of a Christmas programme we would face eight matches, including three against the favourites for the title. United had a bigger squad than us – not better, but bigger. All sorts of permutations enter your mind and converge when you face this kind of crowded, yet so critical, fixture list.

I've always preached, though, that the League was the real test so, come what may, the players knew I would not be hiding any feelings – just maintaining the line I've always peddled with them. Great emphasis was placed on the cup-ties being one-offs. You prepare as well as you can, play as well as you can, you hope you get as lucky as you can but don't get carried away whatever the outcome. Sadly, the history book will show that we were left with the massive challenge of restoring confidence after a pair of cup exits that could have destroyed the whole equilibrium of our season.

The League game at Elland Road came first on 29 December. Three days earlier the Mancunians had trounced our bogey team, Oldham, 6-3 at Boundary Park. Oldham manager Joe Royle was unstinting in his praise for United after that display and, after we had drawn successive games against Tottenham and Nottingham Forest, Alex's team had climbed above us at the top.

The contrast between our Boxing Day fortunes could hardly have been greater. We threw away a 3-1 lead against a struggling Southampton side and by conceding two goals in the closing three minutes ended up with another draw. It was galling and I made it clear in the privacy of the dressing-room and, on this occasion, publicly that we could not afford this kind of charitable approach to our season.

In recent years the games we've staged beteen United and Leeds have been a credit to football. There is immense rivalry and yet nobody has attempted to take this beyond an acceptable point and into the murky waters of vendettas. That assessment was justified by the fact that in four vital matches between the clubs last season there was just one caution. The atmosphere inside the ground – be it Elland Road or Old Trafford – is always electric and yet you can still witness a basic honesty in the way each team has pursued success.

Neil Webb drove home a right-footed shot from 20 yards to give the visitors the lead when we had only half-cleared a left-wing corner. Television replays suggested that Brian McClair had been caught in an off-side position in front of goal as our back line pressed out but the goal was given and became another little set-back in the run of bad luck we were experiencing at the time.

We deserved some reward for our endeavours and it came late in the game when Gary Pallister bundled Gary McAllister to the ground to concede a penalty. Pallister had a series of outstanding performances against us and I believe those displays, featured as they were on television, played a major role in helping him win the support of the players' union as the PFA's Player of the Year. The pressure was on the penalty-taker but Mel Sterland stepped forward and drove his shot past Peter Schmeichel to clinch our fourth consecutive League draw.

The League table at the turn of 1991 made interesting reading and emphasised precisely why, at that stage, the odds were being reduced by the day on Manchester United winning the title.

	P	W	D	L	F	A	Pts
1 Man Utd	21	14	6	1	42	14	48
2 Leeds Utd	23	12	10	1	39	18	46

A two-point lead and the possibility of extending their superiority to eight points thanks to games in hand made them an attractive bet to many punters. At that stage they were also out-scoring us and on course to shatter League records by breaking through the 90-point barrier for the season. We could not allow ourselves to become overawed by the immediate opposition – but that was an easier argument to wage before we had been knocked out of both the Rumbelows League Cup and FA Cup by them.

The Rumbelows Cup may not enjoy the tradition or glamour of the world's premier knock-out competition for clubs but the fact that we were staging a quarter-final at Elland Road with the prospect of facing lower division opponents in the semi-finals made the old-style League Cup an attractive proposition to us. Leeds had not appeared in a Wembley final since the 1973 upset of losing the FA Cup to Sunderland and the reward for our long-suffering supporters, as well as the obvious cash injection to the club coffers, made a trip to Wembley abundantly appealing. After the drawn League game I set my sights on winning the quarter-final and relished having a genuine tilt at reaching the Twin Towers.

Predictably, both line-ups were the same but on this occasion we took the lead through a well-worked effort from Gary Speed. It was just the start we needed and the onus was on us to see the job through. United's lifeline came from Clayton Blackmore's long-range free-kick. Everyone knows the Wales international packs a powerful shot but I was still surprised when he caught Lukic and our defence napping with his right-foot strike from 30 yards.

At this stage of the season I felt United had developed a formation for away games that suited their personnel particularly well. They revelled in the counter-attacking approach that lent itself to their travels with blistering pace on the wings from the Ukrainian Andrej Kanchelskis and Wales starlet Ryan Giggs. Mark Hughes was a brave focal point for their attacks and Brian McClair seemed to revel in a free role switching between midfield and attack. McClair has the stamina to continually make supporting runs from deep positions and probably gets on the end of more goal-scoring chances from there than if he is sent to play as an out-and-out striker. Shackling McClair was a problem many teams encountered at this time.

Given their pace in attack United didn't need to throw full-backs forward in pursuit of goals or crossing options so their back line was tight. At this time Bryan Robson was fighting against his recurring calf injury so Neil Webb was deployed as the midfield passer while Paul Ince used his high energy level to tackle opponents and make supporting runs.

It was Kanchelskis who turned the tie United's way. Early in the second half he left his wing beat, ran through the heart of our defence and tucked his shot past Lukic. It has to be stated that in all our matches against United left-back Tony Dorigo acquitted himself well. He must consider himself particularly unlucky to be around on the England scene at the same time as such an inspirational and established performer as Nottingham Forest's Stuart Pearce. There have been times when I considered Dorigo's performances as 'impeccable' and yet Pearce has established himself in the England team and must rate as one of the few automatic choices manager Graham Taylor can make.

Even though he recognises he is an understudy nobody can doubt Tony's commitment to the England cause. There was much debate last season about the club versus country issue. My views are quite plain. International duty for a player is a duty, a privilege, an honour and, at times, can be a welcome break from club commitments. For a club manager it can be a nightmare but it's one of those nightmares I'm happy to endure. If a player is fit he should be allowed to represent his country. I would never attempt to dissuade him. In fact, there were times during the race for the title when I felt it was beneficial for the likes of Dorigo and Batty to head off with England, Strachan and Gary

McAllister to be involved with Scotland and Gary Speed absent to be with Wales. The international breaks took their minds off club matters.

On the other hand, we actually suffered a set-back when Gordon Strachan's mystery back problem flared up on one of his tartan shirt trips abroad. Unfortunately, it was to prove a lingering handicap for the rest of the campaign. But I've always found Scotland coach Andy Roxburgh to be tremendous in respect of monitoring the fitness of the players in his charge before, during and after games. He takes great care to inform you of any problems. However, there are times when complications are unavoidable.

To be fair to Manchester United, they thoroughly deserved their Rumbelows Cup victory against us, which was rounded off by a Giggs' goal. We may not have been happy with the result – or our performance – but we could not complain about the outcome.

The route to Wembley I had mapped out for Leeds duly came to pass for our Pennine rivals. They faced Second Division Middlesbrough in the two-legged semi-final before heading to the final and defeating Nottingham Forest. I'm not trying to demean their achievement but I did believe the winners of our quarter-final tie were likely to win the competition.

Our FA Cup-tie was a third round meeting and therefore so far from Wembley you could look no further than trying to regain pride after the recent cup blow. Seven days had elapsed since the Rumbelows Cup-tie. During the interim United had beaten Everton 1-0 at Old Trafford while we had travelled to Hillsborough and hammered Sheffield Wednesday 6-1. Obviously, to take Leeds back to Hillsborough for the first time since I had left was a big day for me and the other people with a Wednesday connection. I'm sure Mel Sterland, Lee Chapman and Carl Shutt felt the same way.

Chappy was returning to the ground where his own football renaissance really began. He scored a hat-trick which

I'm sure was particularly sweet for him. The one disappointment surrounding our memorable Yorkshire derby victory
had been a caution I had received for allegedly using foul and
abusive language. I deal with that delicate matter, and the
fact that a little piece of football history was made when I
cleared my name, elsewhere, but, despite this disciplinary
problem, we went into the FA Cup meeting with United in
good spirit.

I think it's fair to rate our performance in this game as our
best against United in the eight times the teams met during
our first couple of seasons back in the top flight. The critical
factor was that we couldn't make the breakthrough and,
thanks to another breakaway goal engineered down the left-
wing by young Giggs, Hughes's downward header gave them
the lead just before the interval.

Nobody could fault our determined pursuit of an equaliser
in the second half. The visitors' goal took a pounding and
Chapman was disappointed to miss with a couple of good
chances and was also denied by two brilliant saves from
Peter Schmeichel. Chappy's match was to end in agony
though. It was one of those occasions when Chappy sees the
ball and deals with the consequences later. He stretched to
meet a right-wing cross and, with Pallister bumping into
him, fell awkwardly towards the post and fractured his wrist.
Being knocked out of both domestic cup competitions was
bad enough. Losing our most prolific marksman into the
bargain was a severe set-back with potentially disastrous consequences for the rest of the League campaign.

I also felt great sympathy for our midfielder, Gary
McAllister. On that night he turned in a vintage performance – controlling and passing the ball long and short. He
had really started to show how much he had improved since
joining Leeds from Leicester City in the summer of 1990.
Football has nice parts and nasty parts and good players can
deal with both. If I'm taking any credit for the blossoming of
McAllister I must also take my share of the blame for the one

thing that has gone wrong – the fault he seems to have developed when setting his sights to shoot for Leeds. Powerful, accurate shooting was a feature of his game. Unlike his golf, it's not up to par – but we're working at it.

Chapman has all the qualities of a great goal-scorer. He is single-minded, astute and, out of necessity, fairly thick-skinned. He has endured the taunts of fans and critics for many years only to invariably have the last laugh. I don't think Lee would earnestly demand acclaim in football's hall of fame but he does deserve recognition as a player who has recognised his strengths and strived manfully to exploit them and also improve the areas where he's deficient. Having the intellect to scrutinise your own game is a vital commodity for a footballer. Chapman went through a torrid time at Arsenal and later Sunderland but he became a wiser man for those troubles.

Lee's powers of recovery are also impressive. Few people will forget the horrific fall he had at White Hart Lane a couple of years ago when he slid, head first, along the shale running track. He required plastic surgery to clean up the damage and repair a gaping wound on his forehead yet when the Rumbelows League Cup semi-final against Manchester United arrived eight days later, Chappy was determined to play.

I would never force a player to turn out in these circumstances and it was only after a stringent medical check that Lee received the all-clear. But Chappy's recovery from the broken wrist exemplified his intelligent approach to injuries. He kept himself in good physical trim while his arm was in plaster and then visited the orthopaedic surgeon for an update. There are some players who are naturally cautious and have to put all medical advice to the test before they feel confident to proceed. Chappy listened to the medical verdict, believed what he had been told and willingly re-entered the fray. We did have a special lightweight cast made for use in games but this was more a precaution than a necessity.

It's ironic that at the time we signed Chapman from Nottingham Forest we were being linked with some of the top strikers in the country with £2 million fees being bandied about as the minimum we would have to pay. Chappy cost Leeds just £400,000. Given our experience together at Sheffield Wednesday, I knew exactly what to expect from him. I don't think he has let anyone down and, at that money, he has proved a real bargain.

The announcement of Cantona's arrival was made immediately after our game against Notts County. It's always nice to create a surprise for my friends in the media and some of them appeared quite stunned when I insisted the tall, swarthy Frenchman at my side in the Press room was a certain Eric Cantona, our new signing. Understandably, Eric's recruitment deflected the focus of attention away from our 3-0 victory over County – but it was a significant day. I'm sure the fans present and David Batty will never forget his super solo goal and that victory extended our unbeaten run to 16 games, the best sequence since I had joined the club.

No matter how hard you try to maintain a sensible approach within your club there are inevitably moments that test the calmest demeanours. Transfer speculation is one of those subjects that I used to get wound up about. I now prefer to leave people guessing until I'm ready to publicly play Leeds United's hand. I've found that is the best way to deal with the matter.

When the transfer deadline was approaching last March we were inevitably supposed to be signing a whole host of players, with Feyenoord centre-back John de Wolf heading our way for £2.3 million while Gary McAllister was reputedly moving to Glasgow Rangers in a £3 million transfer. There was no truth in either assertion but I was disappointed when told that the McAllister fairytale emanated directly from a rival First Division manager's Friday Press conference the day before we were scheduled to play Wimbledon.

Obviously, one never knows the absolute truth in these matters; however I don't think you should seek to destabilise a club in a job that's already hard enough. The most rewarding aspect was that far from unsettling Gary the opposite occurred and he duly produced his best display for weeks in our 5-1 victory.

By this stage of the season we were able to concentrate on our League programme while Manchester United were knocking aside Middlesbrough in the two-legged semi-finals and heading to Wembley to appear in the Rumbelows Cup final. You crave stability within your squad, and we were grateful that, despite being sidelined for seven weeks, Chapman had only missed five matches. You then face the sort of bloody spectacle that blighted our home match against Aston Villa.

Within the opening five minutes we had two defenders off the field requiring stitches and treatment to head wounds. It was incredible. Chris Fairclough and Mel Sterland were involved in the kind of aerial collisions that happen so often in games without any consequence. We had to play for a spell with just nine men and Batty and Strachan were quite brilliant, at this juncture, playing keep-ball as I hoped to be able to regain our starting line-up, if possible. Unfortunately, Chris had to be withdrawn and we sent on John McClelland but Mel did manage to see out the match. Inevitably, the extra workload and disruption caused by the injuries took their toll. It wasn't our most inspired performance but when we were awarded a penalty late in the game I thought Gordon Strachan would clinch us three points.

Villa keeper Nigel Spink was a man with a mission that night. He had become disheartened following a long spell out of the team as Les Sealey's deputy. He had seized the opportunity to prove his worth in emphatic style by producing a string of superb saves. The one we didn't need was from Gordon's spot-kick. It wasn't the skipper's best effort but Spink guessed right and ensured the game ended goal-less.

The victory we wanted didn't materialise and the odds continued to favour Alex Ferguson's team.

There was a genuine danger that the title race might be polarised into a public debate involving predictions of glory from Leeds and Manchester United. I was determined that would not be the case in the Elland Road camp. The final 12 games of the campaign were going to be fascinating. We had never dropped out of the top two places and I was still convinced, despite Manchester United's continued progress, that the 82 to 84 points target might just clinch the crown. We had a players' meeting and I suggested that we set no new targets and forget about League points. I asked them again to focus even more on performances. I made the comparison between football and golf. We had played three rounds and were entering the final day, final round of a major tournament. We were up at the top of the leader board with little between us and our main rivals. It was a case now of who could produce the best score. We couldn't afford to tighten up, we must not get too cocky. The swing that we'd worked on and perfected had to be trusted. We had to prepare ourselves properly then go out and play our shots. 'Trust your swing', was the advice I repeated constantly.

I also told them that my worrying was finished. I had done all that work in pre-season training to cover every angle. I'd done my barking, badgering and, on occasions, bullying. I told them that provided they performed to their own standards to the end of the season they could not fail.

Joe Frazier, the former world heavyweight champion and great rival to the incomparable Muhammad Ali, summed up my assessment of our situation when he claimed, 'If I lose I will walk away and never feel bad because I did all I could – there was nothing more to do.' It was vital that, whatever the destiny of the Championship crown, we were left with no aftertaste of what might have been. We had to give the title our very best shot. If we won it we could bask in the glory of heroes. More importantly, if we came second we would walk away with our heads held high, sure in the belief that this might not be our season but nobody could ask any more of us.

Undoubtedly, Manchester United paid the price for their own success. It was an unfair workload to expect them to fulfil five crucial League matches in the space of ten days in the wake of winning the Rumbelows Cup. I mention elsewhere that, of any club, Leeds should sympathise with the Mancunians' plight. After all, Leeds had seen their football dreams shattered in this very way so often in the past during Don Revie's era.

A good result at White Hart Lane, where we beat Tottenham largely against the run of play, was followed by a disastrous 4-1 drubbing at Queen's Park Rangers. We played poorly and lost Chris Whyte who was sent off for a 'professional foul'.

Despite Sheffield Wednesday's storming climax I honestly couldn't see the title ending up anywhere outside Elland Road or Old Trafford. I remember, around this time, being interviewed by a sports journalist I hold in high esteem, Ken Jones of *The Independent*. Ken had a notion that Leeds would win the Championship and I pointed to the three imminent, and particularly difficult, away games we faced. We had to travel to Arsenal, Manchester City and Liverpool. We were having to patch up the team following the loss of Mel Sterland, who had sustained a nasty ankle injury. Yet again, the ever-willing Speed acted as a short term deputy before Jon Newsome impressed us all with his poise in the final run-in. At the same time, I constantly preached that Manchester United's five games in ten days programme might have a major bearing for us.

We brought a deserved point back from Highbury although it was not as edifying a spectacle for the television cameras as previous Leeds matches. Much as I would have liked the players to turn on a wonder show there are times when you are caught without the cover of make-up, warts and all. As viewers will no doubt discover when they sub-scribe to BSkyB's pay channel soccer for live games, 'You pay your money but you don't always get your choice.'

Our 4-0 defeat at Manchester City was a severe blow. I told the players in the meeting where we mapped out the run-in and Eric Cantona's new role in it, that I was scared they might behave like spoiled kids. They had entered a race but when it seemed they might not win it, they wanted to drop out. They seemed to think second was nowhere. It may be a common theory these days but we had to rally again and prove our worth as a unit. We had to battle on for our own sense of pride and also to exploit any opening brought about by Manchester United's mistakes. Thankfully, in retrospect, both those factors came into play.

Strachan's role as skipper was more crucial than ever before. Above everything else, Gordon's great asset is his quick-thinking. His football brain has been so important to us. We needed him out there on the pitch, despite his troublesome back problems, and guiding us through the demands of a title run-in. Manchester United were also facing critical times. If they failed to cash in from their games in hand we needed to be ready to pounce, but con-versely, if we didn't keep accumulating points our pursuit would be in vain.

Chelsea were the next visitors to Elland Road and Strachan's brain power created two goals. A quick throw-in was seized by Cantona who flicked the ball over Paul Elliott, and swayed past another defender before rifling a cross-shot into the top corner for the sort of goal Roy Race would be happy to claim for Melchester Rovers. It was a goal that was deservedly shown all over the world that weekend. After beating Chelsea 3-0, the next few days were crucial as we prepared for the trip to Anfield. But just 48 hours later we would have to face Coventry on Easter Monday and I decided that kind of programme might prove too much for Gordon Strachan. Michael Hennigan and I called Strach in to discuss the run-in and of the four remaining matches I pointed out that we were likely to see more of the ball in the games against Coventry, Sheffield United and Norwich. I explained my thinking, confident that he would not be troubled by the responsibility resting on his shoulders. We could not afford to lose at Anfield, it was as simple as that. Psychologically, gaining even one point would be vital.

Gordon understood the scenario and agreed to go along with the plan. He would miss the Liverpool trip but, hopefully, play in all the remaining games. Lukic was brilliant in goal at Anfield. He produced some superb stops which was just as well with Rush and Saunders in incisive mood and Jan Molby spraying passes around midfield. They say you have to be daft to be a goalkeeper. I think different would be a better word – and John is definitely different. He is known around the club as 'Lukey' but he should be known as 'Cool Hand' from the Paul Newman film. He certainly doesn't get too excited about his performances. Over those final few weeks of the season he definitely bore the hallmarks of a man who'd seen it all before with Arsenal. I'm not sure that the ice-cool approach comes quite as naturally as he would like us believe but I know his attitude to the week's training is geared towards Saturday. He has very fixed ideas about his training and being fit for the match. It's not always everyone's ideal but I feel that kind of individualism, when backed by good intentions and well reasoned, can help certain people produce their best form. Certainly, Lukey has done that for Arsenal and Leeds.

I deliberately under-played his performance at Anfield. When referring to his splendid saves I chose to quote Brian Clough who, on numerous occasions when talking about Peter Shilton, said, 'That's what I pay him to do.' I meant no disrespect to John but I did not believe it was in the interests of the team to focus on their match-saving goalie. I still maintain, though, that his display at Anfield was why I bought him and why we pay his wages.

The old soccer cliché says, 'Take every game as it comes.' There should be a new one that goes, 'Don't over-react when hailed or hammered by the media.' With the tension at the top of the League reaching breaking point in some people's minds, a draw at Anfield was supposedly a major disappointment in our title quest. I walked out of Liverpool on that afternoon a happy and relieved man. There was a tangible feeling inside Anfield that they would make life very difficult for their next visitors, Manchester United. Some of the players heard shouts from the famous Kop that they preferred Leeds to win the Championship more than their rivals from down the East Lancashire Road. I was satisfied that gaining even one point might prove difficult for Fergie's boys.

The absence of Strachan left many pundits bewildered. I was challenged as to how I could be so stupid to omit such an influential player. I was accused of making the blunder that would cost Leeds the title and one famous ex-player, John Giles, in the *Daily Express*, was particularly scathing. The key issue was that we now had three games remaining and I sensed we could win all three.

United still held the edge and on 18 April remained in pole position.

	P	W	D	L	F	A	Pts
1 Man Utd	38	20	15	3	59	27	75
2 Leeds Utd	39	19	16	4	68	35	73

The public interest in our battle at the top had reached fever pitch. The biggest League crowd of the season, some 47,576 spectators, packed inside Old Trafford on Easter Monday to view United's match against Nottingham Forest, a welcome opportunity for revenge for Brian Clough's team after their Rumbelows Cup final defeat. Our home game against Coventry had been delayed to allow maximum television impact, so just minutes before we went out for that vital encounter we knew that Forest had done us a massive favour by winning 2-1 at Old Trafford.

I don't totally agree that knowing the Old Trafford result made our immediate task easier. The news from Manchester was not just privy to our players. Everyone inside Elland Road knew we would climb above United again by defeating Coventry and that piled immediate pressure on our players from the start. Yet again we confronted a goalkeeper in big Steve Ogrizovic who seemed more inspired than intimidated by his visit to Elland Road. There was no doubting the passion of the crowd and their desperation at seeing us win. We were therefore grateful when Chris Fairclough popped up to send a looping header over Ogrizovic to score his third goal of the season.

Gary McAllister claimed our second from the penalty spot but we again witnessed a harsh sending-off when Lloyd McGrath was adjudged to have stopped a Cantona shot with his hand. I would concede that the penalty award was debatable. Dismissing McGrath was needless. In fact, Eric should have spared the Coventry player that indignity by converting the glorious goal-scoring opportunity with the panache we had grown to expect from him.

I headed to the home dressing-room after that victory and saluted the players for achieving our target for the season. We were now assured of a place in the UEFA Cup. I sensed some of them might have thought my congratulations were just a ploy. To a degree they were, but I didn't want them to feel under any pressure at all. After all, qualifying for Europe was the ambition I had set myself and mentioned to the directors. The Chairman and his boardroom colleagues were delighted that the aim had been fulfilled. Anything else would be a bonus and Manchester United still had that game in hand on us.

It came quickly for them, just 48 hours later at West Ham, a club that had been dogged all season by problems on and off the field and looked certain to be relegated. The common perception seemed to be that I would want to head to Upton Park and personally witness the outcome of such a critical game. I disagreed. Our reserve team had a match against Bradford City. There was nothing I could do by travelling to London that might affect the outcome. It turned out to be a good night all round though, because the reserves won 5-2 and West Ham pulled off a critical 1-0 win. I actually recall climbing into my car and setting off for home on that night. The live commentary of the United match was on the radio and I switched on to hear the 1-0 scoreline with the game still in full flow. I immediately switched off and slipped in a cassette tape. I just didn't want to get involved in that result in any way until I absolutely had to.

We were top by one clear point and with both teams having played 40 matches. Every possible permutation was worked out. The one conviction I maintained was that the race would go to the wire. That was the prediction I had made weeks earlier to the players within the privacy of the dressing-room.

I was wrong. Four days later the day of reckoning arrived. This time it was Leeds who had to kick off early and attempt to gain the initiative before Manchester United appeared in their televised match at Liverpool. We also knew that if we could win this one it would leave United having to gain a victory at Anfield.

Our game against Sheffield United will never be remembered for its flowing football, great goals or fine skills. It was a Yorkshire derby battle that might have had more in common with a Third Division match than the one that would see us win the title. But on days like these you can only concern yourselves with results and we won 3-2. There were ricochets, defensive howlers and own goals. Thankfully, luck was very definitely on our side.

It was somehow fitting that an ex-Wednesday player should not only star for Leeds that day but score. Young Newsome, totally belying his tender years and inexperience, was superb at right-back and popped up with our second goal. What a bargain he was proving. There was a mounting belief in the visitors' dressing-room at Bramall Lane, and in the boot-room where my mate, stingy Harry Bassett serves that cheap Spanish champagne, that the race for the title was all over. So it proved.

We had enjoyed a marvellous season and the rivalry between the two clubs at the top was healthy and full of respect. Perhaps the crucial difference over that second half of the season can be seen in the 'goals for' column of the two sides. Our final match against Norwich was a formality. As far as I was concerned, expectations had certainly exceeded the realisation. If it had not been disrespectful to the game it would have been appropriate to play some of the lads who had made it all possible by their hard work in the early days when, against tremendous odds, we had dug our way out of Division Two and removed the taint of dishonour that had become synonymous with the name of Leeds United.

Peter Haddock, my player of the year when we were promoted, had to deal with the cruel blow of shattering his knee ligaments in the Littlewoods Cup semi-final against Manchester United. At the time he was on the verge of being recognised as a First Division player. Mervyn Day had to sit there week-in, week-out watching Lukic enjoy life in the top grade. Mike Whitlow, Bobby Davidson, Chris Kamara and Imre Varadi, Glynn Snodin and even Dylan Kerr, had at one time or another, played their part.

Form since 29 December 1991:

	P	W	D	L	F	A	Pts
1 Leeds Utd	19	10	6	3	35	19	36
2 Man Utd	21	7	9	5	21	19	30

Our triumph was emphatic. We eventually finished four points clear. We had won more matches than any other team in the First Division and lost fewer. Only one team, Arsenal, had out-scored us. We will never be able to prevent debates about the merits of a particular season but nobody can doubt when they scrutinise the final League table that we proved ourselves the best team over football's very own marathon.

Behind the scenes we don't have the biggest staff in football but that week we all enjoyed the celebrations. When you're born and bred in South Yorkshire, though, you are never allowed to get carried away by success and there's a gateman at Barnsley who must have been revelling in telling his own personal Wilkinson anecdote in the aftermath of our Championship success.

I was manager of Sheffield Wednesday at the time and we had a reserve team match at Oakwell. I left my vehicle on that mountain-side car park which should carry a government health warning for exhaust pipes. I bought the obligatory scratch-off lottery cards from the lovely lady who marshals the car park entrance and headed for the official entrance. I was confronted by a chap who might have walked straight out of an Al Read, or better still, a Barry Hines script. He was wearing a flat cap and red and white muffler. 'Where's tha think tha's gooing?' he asked, with usual Yorkshire hospitality.

'I'm Howard Wilkinson,' I replied, somewhat embarrassed.

Obviously warming to his task and sensing my unease he enquired, 'Tha's who?'

'Howard Wilkinson, manager of Sheffield Wednesday,' I maintained.

They say there are perks to every job and with one sideways glance he dismissed me as an impostor, announcing, 'Aye, lad, and I'm Arthur Scargill. Next door please and it'll cost you two quid to get in.'

On my last visit to Oakwell my friend was still there. He has mellowed somewhat. These days I usually get, 'Come in here, no charge, Howard.' But I bet he's guaranteed free drinks for years at my expense. Maybe we should have sent him a bottle of bubbly after Leeds had won the League.

Final leading positions:

		P	W	D	L	F	A	Pts
1	Leeds Utd	42	22	16	4	74	37	82
2	Man Utd	42	21	15	6	62	33	78
3	Sheff Wed	42	21	12	9	62	49	75
4	Arsenal	42	19	15	8	81	46	72
5	Man City	42	20	10	12	61	48	70
6	Liverpool	42	16	16	10	47	40	64

Chapter 2

THE TEARS AND THE CROWN

'Same canoe, same paddles and the same bloke in charge'.

On the face of it my move to Leeds was crazy. I was manager of Sheffield Wednesday, who were seventh in the First Division, while mulling over the chance of joining a once great club that was, at that time, languishing four places off the foot of Division Two. There was a genuine danger that Leeds were heading for Division Three and taking me with them.

Leeds' status as the most unpopular club in England, a reputation that had escalated over three decades, also concerned me. The hostility towards the club in playing terms was originally sparked by the ruthless pursuit of success epitomised by Don Revie's team during its formative years. When Revie took the shackles off his truly great side in the early Seventies much of the damage had already been done. The public perception of the club had been formed. Many people, with closed minds, were loathe to review their opinions.

The club had also attracted an undesirable lunatic fringe, some of the worst offenders actually commuting to matches from Scandinavia. As Leeds' status as a European power grew so did the element of fans who latched onto the club for the wrong reasons. Overall, the club had been tainted by the misdemeanours of the past. We faced a massive challenge to earn the right to a fresh start and, hopefully, to win public acclaim for all the right reasons.

The decision to join United was not an easy one. From the moment Wednesday chairman Bert McGee informed me that he had given Leeds permission to approach me there had been many sleepless nights. Football being what it is there had been abundant rumours, phone calls and badly disguised speculation. But I remember travelling up the M1 on a Friday afternoon to meet Leeds Chairman Leslie Silver after taking training at Hillsborough. It was a wet, miserable day and, in some respects, a journey I did not enjoy making and a meeting I had not looked forward to.

Prior to that meeting with Mr Silver and managing director Bill Fotherby, though, I took the time and trouble to find out as much as I could about the composition of the Elland Road board. I knew the size of each director's stake in the club, his personal business interests and his influence on the running of Leeds United. That knowledge allowed me to take the offensive relative to what I believed Leeds needed to do to enjoy a bright tomorrow. I could sense the Leeds hierarchy were taken aback by my information and attitude.

It had been Fotherby's task to make the initial approach and convince me I should meet his Chairman. Bill arrived at my home looking nothing like any director I'd ever worked for and, I have to admit, my first impressions were cool. He was flamboyant, some might say loud, but was unstinting in his enthusiasm for Leeds United. His belief in the club was absolute and total. He would not rest until he had convinced me that it was with Leeds that I could achieve all my ambitions as a manager.

I agreed to meet Leslie Silver and on an autumnal afternoon we sat through the twilight and on into the night as the talk about the renaissance of Leeds bounced around his office. I spelt out the three routes I believed a club could take in an attempt to reach the First Division and, even more importantly, aim to make its mark at the highest level. I had charted this precise course with Wednesday and, to my mounting frustration, failed to win the financial backing from the boardroom I felt was imperative to see the job through properly.

The statistics are there for all to see. A newly promoted club in the top flight has a life-span of only around five years unless solid, sound investments in new players are established as top priorities. Failure to accept this principle has seen so many clubs, including the likes of Manchester City, Chelsea and West Ham, become footballing yo-yos, up and down by virtual rota. I did not want that to become Leeds' blueprint for the future.

I outlined my three soccer scenarios. The least attractive, or route three, involved a club with no money to spend where we lived a hand-to-mouth existence and by hard work hoped to pull off the kind of miraculous success enjoyed during my days at Notts County. Promotion to Division One in those circumstances was an unfair challenge but it could be done with the right mixture of players and backroom staff and a healthy degree of good fortune. Leeds' ambitions surely lay above this avenue. The second path involved a middle course where new players, strictly within an ordered budget, could be recruited but again with no promise of an immediate return.

I noticed the Chairman was making notes continuously as I outlined my ideas, leaving until last route one. The board would have to back my judgment by investing in new players and an increased wage bill aimed at taking Leeds up within two seasons of my taking charge. The risk factor in financial terms was enormous but I knew the rewards would prove more than worthwhile. I wanted to accumulate a playing staff that would in the main be able to act as the foundation once the club arrived back in the big time. Again, more investment would have to take place then. It may surprise some people but I actually outlined a ten-year plan for Leeds United, involving the recruitment of schoolboy players and the launch of a new scouting network, as well as the obvious demands for producing a successful League side.

To my astonishment Mr Silver quickly assured me that he saw no deep problems in providing the finances to regenerate Leeds and adopt the most aggressive approach in order to fulfil our joint ambitions. Those words came as music to my ears. Obviously, he insisted, there would have to be stages along the way where he and his fellow directors could assess the validity of my approach. Thankfully, with time, most of what I said has come to fruition and consequently the Chairman's confidence in my advice has grown. In tandem with that development a greater sense of trust has developed between us. And immense credit for what we have achieved must also be heaped on managing director Fotherby and vice-chairman Peter Gilman.

My departure from Hillsborough was still a protracted affair because Bert and I believed it was not in the interests of Wednesday for me to leave until after the shareholders' annual general meeting. There was a faction pressing for changes and I was not going to allow anyone the chance to exploit my departure and embarrass the club. It may have seemed hypocritical of me to defend the Wednesday hierarchy in this manner because their inability to financially support my plans for bringing better, and subsequently higher paid, players to Hillsborough was a constant frustration. However, that was what they believed was best for the club. The club must come first and, in addition to this, Wednesday had come a long way from those dark Third Division days. I wouldn't allow myself to put that progress at risk if I could avoid it.

I was perpetually referred to in some circles as the manager who couldn't sign big name players when the Wednesday pay structure at the time made this totally impossible. In many respects I wanted the Wednesday fans to know and understand my dilemma but a sense of duty to my employers prevented me from publicly exposing a policy

I knew was, in the long-term, short-sighted. Transfer fees were agreed with Southampton for the likes of Mark Wright and Nottingham Forest for Chris Fairclough but matching the financial terms on offer at Derby and Tottenham respectively was impossible and Wednesday were left gasping in their slipstream. I can explicitly recall on three separate occasions explaining within board meetings at Hillsborough the imperative need to review financial planning and outlining the path I thought the club should be heading down. On all three occasions I failed to win the necessary support and eventually I realised Leeds, despite their League status at the time, were a club capable of matching and then surpassing anything Wednesday might achieve. Wednesday became known as 'the big city club with the small town mentality'. I began to realise the self-imposed handicap the club was operating within.

Wednesday's salary scales and commitment to major transfers has altered in recent years to coincide with changes inside the boardroom. I know my successors, Ron Atkinson and Trevor Francis, have enjoyed the benefits of a more expansive financial approach. Thankfully, the club is now prepared to deal in the real world! To illustrate my argument I would point out that in February 1979 Trevor became the first £1 million footballer when he moved from Birmingham City to Nottingham Forest. Six years to the month later we created Wednesday's record transfer by paying Queen's Park Rangers just £265,000 for Simon Stainrod. I did manage to improve on that twice more by recruiting Garry Thompson and Ian Cranson but the new high of £475,000 was hardly excessive. Yet, even given my genuine grievances, the day I finally departed from Hillsborough was heart-breaking for me.

I spent five minutes talking to the office staff and secretaries before I was close to breaking down and realised I must head for the dressing-room. I then met the players and tried to convey to them that life must go on and that they would succeed without me. Towards the end of that meeting the emotions welling up inside me forced me to walk out and I rushed to the bootroom as a bolthole. I grabbed a large blue towel and sobbed into it for ten minutes. I remember bitterly saying, 'If it wasn't for those bastards in the boardroom I would still be here.' It did me good to get the vitriol out of my system.

There was a time when I genuinely believed I would never leave Hillsborough. I was convinced we were creating something that would last forever. There was an empathy between the players and me and my coaching staff that I believed no other club could match. Before games we held hands in a circle that was meant to mark our coming together as a clan. It was a symbolic act to show we were going out as a team and that the team was as strong as its weakest player. We were dependent on each other and committed to victory. At first some players found it difficult to join the circle but soon it became our talisman.

Like all these things it has its day. There were players who found it embarrassing and they weren't as committed to it. I recall Lee Chapman, whom I signed for both Wednesday and Leeds, asked to be excused. Having said that, until the day I left Hillsborough even I was not aware of the type of feelings and *esprit de corps* my particular style of management could provoke. That was highlighted a few weeks later.

A senior Wednesday player telephoned me and asked if he could meet me privately. A neutral venue at a Sheffield hotel was agreed and I wondered what problems were about to present themselves. When I turned up I was met by a dozen or so Wednesday players who greeted me with a genuine show of affection. They had come to know some of my interests, one of which was antiques, and had bought me a beautiful, solid silver, Victorian petit-four dish. I drove away from the farewell party wondering if we would have achieved even more if I had known the real depth of their commitment to our cause. The knowledge and relationship

I had built up with so many players at Hillsborough inevitably spilled over into my career at Leeds. I signed a
couple of youngsters in Jon Newsome and David Weatherall
as well as an old stager in Imre Varadi direct from Wednesday while there were others like Chapman, Mel Sterland and
Carl Shutt who arrived at Elland Road by a more circuitous
route. The list might have grown longer if I could have
persuaded various Wednesday managers to part with other
key men.

The blunt truth was that the foundation stone to
Wednesday's success was invariably perspiration rather than
inspiration. On a sliding scale of ten we had to compete in
matches at the level of nine to achieve anything. Any dips
below that mark in terms of endeavour and we were in
trouble. After two or three seasons of continuous improve-
ment it became clear that, despite increased attendances, the
club could not fund the recruitment of players capable of
really winning things. There were so many near misses. We
were bankers each season to reach at least the last eight of
the cup competitions but the silverware so painfully eluded
us. You could argue forcibly that within the structure of
investments and wage scales the players had done the club
proud but you are then overlooking the dream syndrome in
football – the desire of every fan that his team will win a
major trophy. Arthur Hopcraft put it most succinctly when
he wrote, 'The football fan is not just a watcher. His seat,
and his nerves work on football, and his spirit can be made
rich or destitute by it.' Having grown up in Sheffield, I knew
the hunger for success that existed among the Hillsborough
faithful . . . and how I wanted to satisfy them.

The big breakthrough proved elusive to us although I
think we all believed we were right on the brink in 1985-86.
Our League form was impressive and while we didn't
deserve to be tipped as Champions-elect in the autumn, as we
were by one irrational critic, we never dropped lower than
ninth position and eventually finished a highly creditable

fifth. Liverpool, in the first season after the Heysel stadium tragedy, emerged as Champions.

The UEFA ban on English clubs competing in their tournaments was a bitter blow but the FA Cup still offered us the chance to see Wednesday win their first trophy since 1935 when they defeated West Bromwich Albion 4-2 at Wembley. We had to be at our combative best to force our way past the contemporary West Brom, after a replay, Orient and Derby, again after a replay. The quarter-final against West Ham remains one of the most memorable games during my Hillsborough managerial reign. It was a superb, attacking match which we won thanks to goals from Carl Shutt and Nigel Worthington. Worthy was ribbed for weeks afterwards for scoring with the right foot he usually just stood on. Shutt's effort was a real cracker and our 2-1 victory earned us a semi-final meeting with Everton who, at that time, were reigning Champions and holders of the European Cup-winners' Cup.

If the outcome of one match might have loosened the purse strings and transformed the club policy during my tenure it was that semi-final at Villa Park. The stakes for the club and my plans as manager were so high. We started in impressive fashion and won a series of corner-kicks that invariably in the past had brought us the reward of a goal. From the best chance Gary Megson headed over a Paul Hart flick-on when it appeared easier to find the net.

We had been forced to re-jig our line-up after Brian Marwood had pulled up during training in the build-up to the semi-final at Lilleshall with a hamstring strain. I opted to attack Everton's quick defence with a three man strike force of Lee Chapman, Garry Thompson and Shutt. Ironically, Everton's plans were hit early in the game when Trevor Steven sustained a groin injury and they introduced substitute Alan Harper.

It was Harper who gave them the lead just four minutes into the second half. We believed he was off-side but the linesman disagreed and Harper was through on goal. It was a split-second decision for any goalkeeper but, in retrospect, Martin Hodge would have been better advised to stand his ground and buy time for his rapidly recovering defence. Instead, Hodgey chose to race out and dive low at Harper's feet which, effectively, made the decision easier for the substitute. He kept his nerve to lob the ball calmly over the advancing goalie and into the net.

Given Everton's status at the time and their advantage in possessing players with experience of cup semi-finals and European ties, I knew we needed to hit back quickly or face real problems. Mercifully, the equaliser came to fruition within minutes. It was an opportunist header by Shutt from Hart's downward header and with the game level again the stage was set for a memorable climax.

When people discuss great teams of the modern era you very rarely hear them mentioning that Everton line-up but I have no qualms in citing the midfield axis of Peter Reid and Paul Bracewell as one of the most influential and effective we've witnessed in recent years. They made up a brilliant combination and hunted for possession so effectively as a duo. Skipper Kevin Ratcliffe was then at his fastest before the unfortunate groin injury he sustained at Hillsborough a few years later. And in attack they had Graeme Sharp, a good all-round striker, blessed with the ability to trouble you in the air but also possessing great ball skills on the deck.

I was still quite happy to see the semi-final drifting towards extra-time without a winner. Once we were into the added half hour I believed the Wednesday lads would come strong and snatch victory. Sadly, that plot was ruined by an exquisite volley from Sharp. It may have been fatigue in some legs but after partially clearing a corner we didn't mark tightly enough as the ball was knocked back into the area and the Scotland striker despatched his shot in consummate style.

There were tears of sadness shed after this game. But two incidents within that particular season emphasised in my mind the kind of team spirit Wednesday, at that time, had going for them. The first example occurred off the field, the second very definitely on it.

We organised a Christmas party for the players at a local hotel and invited the journalists, from both local newspapers and nationals, who regularly covered out matches. A list of awards had been drawn up and the players had tendered their nominations for the various categories such as 'The best dressed player', 'The worst dressed player', 'The hen-pecked husband', 'The biggest boozer' etc. We also had a special Press award for the reporter the players believed wrote the most ill-informed copy.

As the adjudicator I then selected a player I knew had not won a particular prize and asked him to bring a suitable award for the victor. Hence, when Lawrie Madden was unanimously voted 'The worst dressed player' he was presented by Harty with an evening dress outfit, including white tie and tails, and was ordered to change into it for the rest of the meal. The final award was to the Press and one of the players had bought a kingsize pair of longjohns to which his wife had sewn a pair of huge lips around the posterior. The 'Speaking through your backside' award was then handed over among great pomp and ceremony to the reporter who a few weeks earlier had tipped Wednesday to win the League.

It was a fun luncheon, with everyone present entering the mood of frivolity in the right way. But it's no good just having a happy ship off the field. There was work to be done on it and the collective reaction to our extra-time defeat gainst Everton also reflected the sense of purpose being generated at Hillsborough.

Some of the wisest old heads in football warned me that our Villa Park set-back was likely to cast a shadow over the rest of our campaign. It would be very hard to rouse the players in the League when they knew the ban on English clubs appearing in Europe effectively negated the spur of aiming for a flying finish to snatch a UEFA Cup berth. It wasn't the easiest of run-ins either with away games at Manchester United and Southampton and tough home fixtures against the likes of Arsenal, Aston Villa and relegation-haunted Ipswich. How I wish the tenacity they displayed in those last seven matches had been rewarded with a Wembley place. As it was, we won five and drew two of the matches to clinch Wednesday's highest League position for 25 years. Ipswich may not have been so pleased by our determination. Their single-goal defeat at Hillsborough on the final day of the season saw them relegated.

We still needed to sign players with the potential to lift Wednesday on to a new plane. Instead, we were left searching on too many occasions for bargain basement buys or players whose careers had been blighted by injury. There were many occasions, especially during the early days, when the budget deals proved very successful. I recall two of my first signings were Martin Hodge, then Everton's third team goalie, for £50,000, and centre-back Lawrie Madden, on a free transfer from Millwall.

By the 1986 World Cup finals in Mexico, Martin had become the stand-by keeper waiting for a late call-up from England and during the same period Lawrie had emerged as one of the quickest defenders in the First Division. He may have had an ungainly running action but it always amused me when the advice from the opposition dug-out to any striker facing Madden was, 'Run him, he's slow.'

After scouring the lower divisions we found winger Brian Marwood at Hull City. We'd watched him for almost a full season and while the really big clubs didn't bite we worked on the basis that Marwood's strengths could be maximised to make him a very effective First Division footballer. He had the ability to move across the front line and find space down the flanks, he was also a good crosser with either foot and could deliver the ball in danger areas. In our overall strategy Brian proved a good acquisition up to his £700,000 transfer to Arsenal.

I had originally worked with a poker-faced Northern Irishman called Nigel Worthington at Meadow Lane. He joined Wednesday for £100,000 and is now on course to launch his testimonial season with them. Nobody could doubt the value for money Nigel has given Wednesday.

We had seasoned professionals like Paul Hart and Gary Owen arriving on free transfers and I suppose my detractors will claim one or two of my bigger buys, relative to Hillsborough, didn't create any tidal waves of success. I did spend a club record £450,000 on striker Garry Thompson and the day before the transaction went through I spoke to one of the old heads I had signed and diplomatically asked his opinion of the potential newcomer, without confirming there was any real Wednesday interest. 'I wouldn't sign him,' was the blunt reply. But we were past the point of no return. Fortunately, Wednesday got their money back 12 months later when Thommo moved to Aston Villa. Garry had never really clicked with us and I'm sure he was happy to get back to the Midlands.

We still managed to unearth some gems outside the First Division and one of those was a precocious 19-year-old called David Hirst, who cost Wednesday just £200,000. We bought David from Barnsley when Allan Clarke was manager and a joke phone call I made to Oakwell almost backfired in dramatic fashion on me. I rang Allan from Hillsborough and proceeded to perform a fairly reasonable impersonation of Peter Shreeves, manager of Tottenham Hotspur at the time. I feigned an interest in young Hirst and realised from his response that Allan had an audience in his office.

He immediately embarked on a long monologue detailing Hirst's virtues, his massive potential and the offers they had already received for him. Before I could interject he was setting up a mega-bucks deal and asking whether I wanted Spurs' interest to be relayed to his Chairman.

I realised the joke was going a bit far and tried to butt in to halt him. He still pressed on until I finally managed to break his flow and explain it was Wilki from Wednesday. Thankfully, Allan saw the funny side then, and still does, but what began as a daft phone call almost got out of hand.

The legend grew that I put Sheffield Wednesday through the most gruelling training sessions in the game. Whenever a senior player was involved in transfer talks he would raise the hoary old chestnut about the cross-country runs and the physical fitness levels. The legend was in fact a myth. It was Alan Brown, manager of Wednesday when assistant-manager Peter Eustace and I were both players, who introduced the idea of taking players away from their day-to-day training environment to offer new surroundings and a fresh approach. Peter remembered that scheme and, given the beautiful countryside within ten minutes' travelling time of Hillsborough, we decided that on the days when the lads would do some running in training we would head for the green and promised lands. In effect, they never did any more training there than they would have done inside the confines of the training ground.

Tony Cunningham, a burly striker, had joined us from Barnsley during our Second Division promotion campaign and on his first cross-country run became a struggling back marker. If the truth be known I still believe he was not helped by certain of his new colleagues, so when he came to the inevitable fork in the path he went to the right while the rest of the squad and management team had turned left. Peter and I waited 45 minutes for him to turn up. Eventually, we gave him up and headed back to Hillsborough only to discover he had been picked up by the police and returned by panda car ahead of us. You can imagine the headlines, 'Nick of time' and all that.

I can't chuckle too heartily at Tony's misfortune because a similar fate was to befall me in Tokyo, of all places, a few years later during a Leeds United trip. We were playing Botafogo of Brazil in a special friendly game at the Tokyo Dome and I decided to go for a run near the team hotel with assistant-manager Michael Hennigan and physiotherapist Alan Sutton. I had the map in my hand as we set off for what was supposed to be an easy 20-minute run. We were out three times as long as we intended as Wilkinson asked directions from a variety of nonplussed Japanese, who didn't speak English and clearly wondered why we weren't hurrying about our business in their manner, during the day. I was politely advised to plot football matches not maps.

Soon after joining Wednesday in that record deal Simon Stainrod, now doing a good job as player-manager at Dundee, was involved in a training run incident that might have had a traumatic effect on his married life. Simon was overweight when we bought him from Queen's Park Rangers and he found it hard to cope with routine training sessions, not to mention games. We had to get him fit and rather than put him through the hard grind of solo sessions some of the backroom staff members would take him for a little run at the end of a normal session in an effort to top up his conditioning gradually.

On this particular day Simon decided to vault a stile in flamboyant fashion. Unfortunately, in mid-air he suffered an attack of cramp in his trailing leg and promptly collapsed only to land, legs akimbo, on the top rail of the stile. The accident didn't do much for his football that week but definitely improved his impersonation of Alan Ball. On such stories are legends born and, to be fair, I think some of the Wednesday lads dined out with their fellow pros for many years on tales of life in the Hillsborough sweat shop. They enjoyed regaling their audience with the fables of Wilkinson's hills, hills and more hills.

There were also many occasions when the laugh was very definitely on me. There was an unforgettable – for all the wrong reasons – trip to Maine Road on Boxing Day 1986 when a good points return over Christmas was set to lift us to second place in the League. Given the stakes I expected a high-class performance from the team. Unfortunately, in the

An ambitious young man on the front row, wide left, with the 1965 Sheffield Wednesday team (© A. Wilkes & Son, West Bromwich)

Training on the seafront at Brighton after consuming the sherry and raw eggs (© Evening Argus, Brighton)

Howard Wilkinson, winger, Brighton
(© Universal Pictorial Press and Agency Ltd, Brighton)

Enjoying my first lap of honour as a manager with Boston United

The FA's new regional coach in 1977

Friendly foes . . . and Notts County had just beaten Bobby Robson's Ipswich Town 3-1 at Portman Road (© Bob Thomas, Northampton)

Alongside my great friend and managerial mentor Jimmy Sirrel with the Notts County squad we took into the First Division in 1981 (© Bob Thomas, Northampton)

Wednesday return to the big time. Physiotherapist Alan Smith, Howard Wilkinson and assistant-manager Peter Eustace celebrate promotion in 1984
(© Steve Ellis, Sheffield)

The face of defeat after losing the FA Cup final to Everton in 1986
(© Steve Ellis, Sheffield)

One of Wednesday's legendary runs in the Yorkshire hills – and Tony Cunningham is nowhere to be seen (© Steve Ellis, Sheffield)

Referees must learn to stamp out physical excesses. Ian Knight is stretchered from the field during Sheffield Wednesday's FA Cup replay with Chester (© Steve Ellis, Sheffield)

Big Jack gets welcomed back to Hillsborough. Howard Wilkinson greets his predecessor as Wednesday manager (© Steve Ellis, Sheffield)

Winning is an obsession and goals are worth celebrating. Howard Wilkinson (© Steve Ellis, Sheffield)

This relay baton should have been collected ten minutes ago.
Howard Wilkinson enjoys a training session (© Steve Ellis, Sheffield)

first half my aspirations were not confirmed. In fact, I didn't think we were really trying to win. We were pussy-footing around and seemingly trying to just survive. To make matters worse, seconds before I could reflect my displeasure, we conceded a goal direct from a free-kick.

At half-time the players arrived in the dressing-room to find Wilkinson in a rage. Now, any manager worth his salt will in quiet moments of reflection admit there is an actor inside him. You occasionally have to be ready to exaggerate your opinions to get the message across in the brief time allowed at the interval. The words of condemnation flowed impressively. 'I'm not pleased with you, your families won't be pleased with you, the fans won't be pleased with you and if God is a Wednesday-ite he won't be pleased either.'

To emphasise the point I then let fly with my left foot and sent a large, but thankfully, empty skip flying across the dressing room. Delighted by that cameo and inspired by the walk on water syndrome of management, I then turned my attention to putting my boot into a medical table . . . and that's where I made my big mistake. The table was fixed to the floor and hard. I crashed my foot against it and felt the pain shoot all the way up my leg. I was in agony and convinced I had, at least, broken my foot.

I couldn't let the players see the damage I had inflicted on myself but there were plenty of smiles in the camp at my expense for the next month while I had treatment and attempted to get over the injury. What did make matters worse was that following the Maine Road defeat I dropped Paul Hart, Gary Megson and Gary Shelton and we still lost to Liverpool in the next match. Our season was to fall away from that point. I have to accept responsibility for the changes I made that, to a degree, led to the disppointing run-in.

When I left Sheffield Wednesday there was obviously a lot of speculation about the possibility of staff moving with me. As it was, Peter Eustace preferred to make his bid for the Hillsborough manager's job on a permanent basis but Michael Hennigan, then Wednesday's youth team coach, declared his intention to move with me and became my number two at Leeds. We had first met when I was the staff coach at an FA full badge coaching course at Loughborough, comprising mainly schoolteachers and one very enthusiastic man from non-League football – Michael. He made a marked impression on me and we eventually teamed up at Hillsborough.

We've formed a successful partnership at Elland Road and much of the success we've enjoyed has been down to him. He gets on with his job, never seeking the limelight or feeling the pangs of frustration so many in his role complain about. And behind the bluff exterior of a South Yorkshireman ticks a very astute brain. He's a shrewd reader of people and situations and I'll never forget the undemonstrative way he turned up at Hillsborough on my final day and, without asking, cleared my desk for me. As we prepared to head for Leeds after those emotional farewells I glumly remarked that I would have to return soon to collect my belongings. Like the character Radar in the film and television programme *M*A*S*H*, Michael explained that the job had already been done and there was no need for me to endure another harrowing trip to the stadium that still held so many fond, and painful, memories for both of us.

But you cannot afford to live in the past. People who live on memories of yesteryear become crushing bores and I was getting the real insight into the size of my challenge at Elland Road. There were so many avenues that needed approaching. The club had an appalling disciplinary record and within my first 18 months at Elland Road I had to attend two FA disciplinary commissions to explain our poor conduct. In those dark days it had become the norm for Leeds to suffer 70-odd cautions in a season and in 1988–89 we had three players dismissed – Ian Baird, John Sheridan and Noel Blake.

A £1,000 suspended fine was invoked along with a further

£3,000 fine but, thankfully, the clean-up programme began to work and the new approach to on-field discipline has reaped its own rewards. In the 1989-90 season we sustained just 34 bookings and we were complimented by the FA for our dramatically improved crime sheet. By last season's Championship campaign we had seen the figure drop to 31 bookings and two dismissals – Leeds' best disciplinary record for 11 years. The crowd problems of the past had been well documented and creating a new, more edifying image for Leeds was an important, some might say critical, part of my approach.

There were times when I wanted to do too many things and I remembered some advice from my old Notts County mentor Jimmy Sirrel. It was Jimmy who climbed on the team bus following a heavy away defeat and announced to the assembled entourage, 'It's back to work on Monday with the same canoe, same paddles and the same bloke in charge.' He was a great advocate that managers should not allow themselves to be side-tracked into cul-de-sacs or waste time on matters that didn't concern them. You must work on the issues over which you have some control or influence. When I asked him once whether my time would be better spent travelling with the reserves to a match or going on a scouting mission he gently counselled that I travel with the second team. 'You can deal with the reserves and help them,' he reasoned. 'You don't know what will happen in the other match. It could be a complete waste of time.'

At Leeds, given my close working relationship on a day-to-day basis with Bill Fotherby, I can concentrate on the varied diet of managing the football matters within the club in the knowledge that Bill, with the Chairman's blessing, can keep abreast with the commercial picture. Football is such big business that employing the best entrepreneurial skills plays a massive part in keeping the team successful on the park.

Until the day I joined Leeds I had always taken jobs and accepted the terms of reference that were put to me. This time experience told me it was for me to dictate the circumstances within which I could accept the post.

I know I've been lucky to date in never having been sacked in football. As a result, I've always been in a reasonably strong position when accepting a new appointment. Obviously, a manager is never fully aware of his own strengths but you learn as you go along. I felt I had learned my lessons. Hence the lengthy negotiations before I moved to Elland Road.

I have always been grateful to be employed but I have adopted an approach to work that I would commend to others. I maintain there are enough shrewd people in executive positions in football to notice when someone, somewhere is doing a good job and deserves credit. Providing you keep faith in your own ability there will always be an employer requiring assistance.

I've been thankful at Leeds to operate alongside managing director Fotherby. He is 'Mr Personality', often everyone's friend but, on some occasions, nearly everyone's enemy. I say that because he tends to be the man who has to introduce the price rises and the unpopular club policies. However, such is Bill's mastery of his craft that in the aftermath of being charged more for their tickets many leave his company apologising for even thinking of complaining.

Gordon Strachan aptly described the Fortherby phenomenon after he had been involved in contract talks with W.J.F. 'I went in for a new contract and came out having purchased a season ticket and apologising for not renting a box.' From the point of view that Bill is a non-footballing executive at the club, I have to state that on a day-to-day basis he has been a greater help to me than anyone else. He has played an invaluable part in the operation that has created the Leeds United success story.

The anecdote that best typifies Bill came in my first season at Elland Road. From the humble launching pad of trying to avoid relegation to Division Three we put together a run that took us into the frame for a promotion play-off place. I sensed we might not have merited that lofty perch but you never turn your back on success in football because it can prove so elusive. Unfortunately, just when expectations were out-pacing reality, we suffered a disappointing home defeat against Crystal Palace.

Despite the fact that I should not have been surprised by our set-back, there was still an air of disappointment around the ground the following day. Bill arrived to find his new manager and assistant-manager staring gloomily at walls in the office. Bill immediately sized up the situation and announced he was taking Michael Hennigan and me for a slap-up lunch at a favourite Italian restaurant in Leeds. Then, throughout a superb meal, he continually reiterated that he wasn't depressed at all by the events of the previous night. On the contrary, he was very excited by the future prospects for Leeds. He was convinced everything was beginning to fall into shape for the future. We had achieved more in a few months at the club than anyone could have expected.

Given the fickle nature of so many relationships in football, experiencing this kind of response when you're down in the dumps means an awful lot to a manager, coach or player. Bill is our daily link with the boardroom but I must also commend Chairman Leslie Silver and Vice-Chairman Peter Gilman for their unstinting support. There has been so much team-work on and off the field and that is the sign of a well-run football club.

Coping with the demands and expectations of directors is an art in itself and one which many young, aspiring managers have to develop. I know, from my own experience, that some of the boardroom operations in my own professional career have been interesting, funny, and, at times, downright ridiculous.

At Boston United nobody had any illusions about who was in charge. During my time at the club we never had a board meeting because Boston was owned and run by one of football's great, unsung heroes, the late Ernest Malkinson. He was an astute businessman who had many fund-raising ideas well ahead of his time. For instance, he was among the first to work at increasing the club's turnover by the sale of games like bingo cards among the supporters. Sadly, careless bookkeeping on behalf of one of his employees at one stage brought Mr Malkinson a *sine die* ban from the Football Association. By the strict letter of the law the ban may have been legally prudent but from a justice point of view it was a mile off-target.

Jim Smith, now the manager at Portsmouth, was my predecessor at Boston and he will confirm that all Mr Malkinson did was pour money into the club. It was his club, his stadium, his players. If bills couldn't be met on time by the club's turnover he made sure the money was available to put the matter right. Board meetings never happened because we had directors in name only to conform with FA and company regulations.

The Chairman's official dealings with the manager would come over a drink following a match. Invariably, the chat would revolve around Mr Malkinson's supporter-like response to the preceding game. After a rare defeat, disappointing draw or poor performance, I would be guaranteed a Monday night phone call at home. The Chairman would have finished his evening meal at around seven o'clock and then ring me. My wife knew the call would last anything from 30 minutes to an hour and a half. It was conversation that came from his heart, a real emotional response to the events of the weekend. There were times when I may have felt like slamming the phone down on him but I never did because I had genuine respect for the man.

Basically, the manager at Boston was left to get on with the job. Invariably, the consultations with Mr Malkinson would revolve around what the manager wanted and how much it would cost. His input was that of a very wise old man who had seen life from all angles. He had flown with the RAF during the First World War: he had built several businesses in the Lincolnshire area from nothing and, despite dallying with showjumping when his daughter Claire was keen on equestrianism, football was his great sporting love.

The transformation, after six years at Boston, to joining Northern Premier League club Mossley was remarkable. Mossley was a lovely club but after attending one board meeting I vowed it would be my last. I walked into the room that was used by the directors to find the assembled delegates sat in two tiers with what seemed three football teams' worth of committeemen, all with a clear opinion on everything that was to be discussed. It was a crazy situation and I told them after my inaugural meeting that in future I would meet two or three selected delegates to discuss any important business.

One of my first away games with Mossley was at Scarborough. I discovered the players were sat three to a seat on the coach to accommodate all the travelling committee men. Indeed, one of the committee men had to stand up for me to gain a seat. There were also committee men sitting on beer crates down the aisle of the coach. The team's form was as unimpressive as the travelling arrangements. We lost the first six games after I took charge. The so-called Messiah from Boston wasn't saving much at this point.

Thankfully, our fortunes did turn and we embarked on a long, unbeaten run to the end of the season, covering 25 games, and eventually won the Lancashire Cup. I left Mossley in a better state than I found them but the FA beckoned to lure me into a job as a staff coach.

Jack Dunnett, later to become President of the Football League, ran the ship his way at Notts County. His special board meeting came at the end of each season when he would invite the manager and his fellow directors to his home for Sunday drinks. The official business would last about 20 minutes as the whole financial business of the year was dealt with, then we would indulge in a pleasant luncheon. Eventually, later that afternoon, we would all say our farewells for the summer and prepare for another 12 months of board meeting-free football.

Jack virtually owned the club and made the executive decisions that mattered. Any discussion between the management and the directors was conducted by him. Jack's departure from football was a loss to the game. He was ousted from the role of League President in one of those interminable power struggles yet, in my dealings with him, I found he had an astute idea of the relationship between directors and managers and some very shrewd ideas for the way forward for the football industry. He was also a politician in both senses of the word. He had been a Labour MP and his moves within football from being involved at Brentford to buying control at Notts represented his political aspirations within the game. I fear it was politics that cost him his lofty position in football's corridors of power.

My time was occupied with board meetings at Sheffield Wednesday more than anywhere else. On average they had eight a year, mainly during the football season, on a monthly basis. The former Chairman Bert McGee used to start them at 7.30 p.m. prompt and, on average, they would last for four hours. As manager I was involved throughout. My views were invited on the whole gamut of the club ranging from catering, building work, auxiliary staff and police charges. There were just seven directors at Hillsborough but at Leeds we're heading towards the remake of the Last Supper with 13 on the board. Invariably, they leave the critical decisions to an executive trio of Silver, Gilman and Fotherby.

I do give a manager's report at the Leeds meetings which occur about once every six or seven weeks. Normally, my input will last no more than five minutes. Questions can be asked but I'm never in the board meetings at Elland Road for more than 15 minutes. My views appertain to the football matters on the field.

Chapter 3

STRACHAN

'For a man so small in size he's a person of great stature.'

Manchester United's FA Cup sixth round defeat against Nottingham Forest in 1989 became one of the most significant and fortuitous days in Leeds United's modern history. Elimination from the Cup provoked Old Trafford manager Alex Ferguson to embark on a dramatic re-building programme and he decided Gordon Strachan was to play no further part in his plans.

I remember the Monday morning vividly. At 9.15 a.m. my secretary Maureen Holdsworth told me Alex was on the phone. To be fair, for the past two years, both with Sheffield Wednesday and Leeds, I had made enquiries to United about the player, so Alex was just keeping me informed that Gordon was now available. He felt events at Old Trafford had come to a head and that the 1-0 home Cup defeat was a signal for him to make radical changes and to try to launch a new era. Strachan would not be part of that new dawn. I could understand the thinking.

I asked him for his valuation and he said the price was £200,000. I immediately called my assistant-manager Michael Hennigan and chief scout Ian MacFarlane into my office to challenge them on whether we should buy Strachan. Both were categoric in backing the plan. They supported my belief that he was a quality player who, to a degree, had been over-shadowed latterly at Manchester United. All clubs have a pecking order, all dressing-rooms have a chain of command and seniority. The Old Trafford dressing-room might have had too many dominating characters, too many good and influential players. In view of skipper Bryan Robson's status with his club and England and his leadership under Ron Atkinson and Alex Ferguson, the time was right for Strachan to move on. Possibly, in many ways, he should have moved earlier.

Anyway, here was a chance for me to obtain the sort of player we needed at Leeds to launch the promotion campaign we knew had to be on the road for the following season. Strachan was to be the famous bloom that would attract some very handsome and hard-working bees to Elland Road. But a start had to be made with a signing of real significance. He fitted the bill to perfection.

I agreed the £200,000 fee with Alex and arranged for the player to travel to Leeds that afternoon. By coincidence, soon after that I received a call from Sheffield Wednesday's then manager, Ron Atkinson. I assumed Ron would be wanting to discuss the players I had left behind at Hillsborough. He was his usual, chatty self and finally came round to the topic of Strachan. He knew the player was available and suggested it wouldn't be in our interests, as a pair of Yorkshire clubs, to get involved in an auction which could only push the price up.

Ron suggested that Wednesday's status as a First Division club and his close relationship from their days together at Old Trafford would prove decisive. He couldn't see Gordon dropping down a division and believed Leeds' involvement might only stimulate the market and, as a result, Wednesday would have to pay more. As a friend he was making me aware of the fact and suggested I politely bow out.

I thanked Ron for his consideration and for his perceptiveness in recognising the way football might let itself down by creating an unsavoury transfer saga. But I was equally determined to pursue my objective and pressed ahead with my plans to meet the player that afternoon. The venue was to be kept secret and no-one was to know of our interest as we met at the home of the Leeds managing director, Bill Fotherby. In fairness, Gordon told us immediately that he was scheduled to speak to two other clubs – Wednesday and Middlesbrough.

The discussions were long and detailed. Occasionally, I would leave the room and Bill would take over. We'd worked out our strategy and we weren't prepared to lose this transfer battle. Deep down we knew it was the right move for all the parties concerned. I see a football club as a family. The team that plays best gets along well too. If you're going to be a successful team out on the pitch it's better that you get on during the week off the pitch. It's not an incestuous situation but it is best if within a football club there is a basis for genuine friendships and respect to flourish. In times of crisis people have to come together and work for a common goal or else your club falls apart.

The better the examples you have within the family, the better chance there is that your youngsters grow up strong and good. I saw Strachan as the perfect example. I had made many enquiries over a couple of years about his character and his way of life and was left in no doubt that he was a man who had become increasingly aware of the need to look after the tools of his trade. He had worked to stay as strong and as fit as possible and as effective as possible too.

If you look after your body your body will look after you and Gordon certainly recognised that maxim. Inevitably, the headlines have tended to refer to his consumption of seaweed pills and bananas but there is much more to the personal fitness programme Gordon pursues than that. Together with his personal fitness guru Harold Oyen, they studied, in minute detail, Gordon's physical and mental fitness and worked out the ways to improve it. Gordon's thorough approach to his job is also reflected by the fact that he retained as important background information his pre-season times for running various distances. This started during his career with Aberdeen and meant that he would never have to seek opinions about his summer fitness levels. He could consult his charts to check his performances and recognise immediately if a problem had begun to emerge. Diet was also important, hence Gordon's zany food intake but, as for his consumption of bananas, I've never seen a fat monkey at any zoo that I've visited!

Before joining Leeds, Gordon had taken an interest in the management side of the game. He had attended coaching courses in Scotland and, while his ideas were fairly embryonic, he had deep-rooted and sensible views about how football should be played. He was a family man. He dealt with the media impeccably and had a great reputation with the staff at Old Trafford for his consideration towards them. Young players at the club also had immense respect for him.

For a man so small in size he's a person of great stature who can destroy at once the big tough guys in the dressing-room with one lash of his coruscating tongue. That's why he deservedly earned the nickname, 'King Tongue'.

When we met I had to make him aware of my knowledge of him and make him realise my plans for him and his role in the re-birth of Leeds. I told him we were certainties to become Second Division Champions, that he would lead us into the First Division and eventually into Europe. Here he was, hoping to hear details of a two-year deal that might have seen out his playing days and being deluged with parts of the exciting masterplan for Leeds' revival. Never in his wildest dreams could he have envisaged the renaissance that was to take place in his career after he joined us.

During our conversation I detected that despite all his past achievements there had crept into Gordon's life an under-current of self-doubt which I picked up straight away. I could see that, like most of us, Gordon needed to be wanted and needed to be associated with worthwhile causes. In no way could he operate in a situation where he felt he had no influence on what went on or where he had fundamentally different views.

We then got down to financial matters and I make no attempt to disguise the fact that the offer we made him left him stunned, or as they say in Yorkshire, gobsmacked. It wasn't a long, complicated contract. It was a deal I estimated would blow all rival offers out of the water. Obviously, he had to talk to his wife Lesley and the other clubs but I felt confident we had prepared the way for his transfer.

He left Leeds to meet Ron Atkinson in Sheffield. We were confident he would be back that very evening as promised to give us his decision in person. There was still the nagging doubt, though, that somehow Ron might work the oracle and persuade Wednesday to go beyond anything they'd paid a player in the past to get Gordon. True to his word, however, Gordon returned at nine o'clock that night looking tired and mesmerised by it all but ready to join Leeds. It's not often you see Gordon stuck for words but he was virtually speechless by this point in an exhausting day.

I know the financial rewards were cited as the big draw for Gordon to join us but I firmly believe that he was swayed by a sense of mission and the affinity he felt for that crusade. He saw the opportunity to be in at the beginning of something big, very much in the vein of Bobby Collins, who had made a similar impression in the development of the great Revie era at Elland Road.

Strachan's was one of the easiest contracts I've ever negotiated. In terms of finance it took 15 minutes. He said he was happy with it and that he would return within 48 hours to complete the transaction. You can imagine my astonishment the next day when Alex Ferguson telephoned to say that United chairman Martin Edwards had received a call at midnight from the Wednesday Chairman to increase their offer for Strachan to £300,000. This was their attempt to price Leeds out of the market and make it impossible for Strachan to join us.

The call had come out of the blue but before Alex had finished talking I told him, 'You've got your £300,000 and if it goes up again we'll match any bid Wednesday make. But knowing you as I do this will be the end of the matter.'

In fairness to Alex it was. He agreed that the deal was done and that the player was happy with our terms. He believed Gordon should travel over to sign for Leeds. The rest, as they say, is history – but what superb history. I've worked with some truly influential players in the past but never one to match the part Strachan has played in my career, or in the development of Leeds.

At Notts County I had Don Masson, whom I inherited from Jimmy Sirrel. Don was another Scot, not a midget but no giant, a great ball artist with fixed views on the game. Like Strachan he was also a great trainer and looked after himself, so it came as no surprise that he could play well into his veteran years. At Meadow Lane we forged a team of unquestionable quality and worked a miracle by taking County and dear old Jimmy Sirrel into the First Division.

At Hillsborough I inherited a totally different type of character as my dressing-room leader. Mike Lyons did not possess the acerbic wit of Strachan or Masson but he was a brave hulk of a man who knew no fear, who shrugged aside injuries and who led by ferocious example. His approach to training, as well as matches, was that of an enthusiastic schoolboy and the players around him respected his unstinting love of the game.

I know there are some managers who fear the influence the powerful dressing-room figures can enjoy inside a club. That is a situation I believe you must accept to reap the benefits of a player who can set standards for the others to follow. Strachan realised we wanted a much deeper association at Leeds than just a senior player with a glowing reputation. We wanted a charismatic influence both on the field and off it.

At first Gordon found some of the things I said fairly radical but he quickly realised I was always willing to sit down and discuss topics and there was inevitably a general agreement on our ideas about football. Professionals are paid to win and the best professionals are paid to win all the time. I know that's not possible but that's the crazy logic all who aspire to be at the very top in football must accept.

I cannot attempt to quantify the job Gordon has done for me. Discipline in hotels on a Friday night has never been a problem; dressing-room debates have never got out of hand. He has represented the players' views fairly and sensibly. He has been a credit to his profession and it was with immense pride that I looked on as Gordon collected the award of 'Footballer of the Year' in 1991 to round off our first season back in the top flight. It could be argued that the football writers were a year late in naming the little man as their out-standing player and the individual who epitomised the best aspects of the game beyond his own inherent ability.

Nobody connected with Leeds will forget Strachan's astonishing contribution to our promotion campaign that culminated in winning the Second Division Championship in 1990. Cast off by Manchester United the previous season, there were times when he carried our team on his shoulders and made sure we fulfilled our ambitions. When the heat of the promotion battle was at its fiercest Strachan even managed to step up another gear. Remember the vital match against Leicester City in our penultimate outing. After Mel Sterland had given us the lead we were pinned back by a superb 20-yard drive from Gary McAllister who, ironically, would sign for us just a few weeks later. We needed a victory to keep us at the top of the division and maintain our status as favourites for promotion. While energy and courage were draining from those around him Strachan took up the gauntlet and ran forward. His face and his every physical movement betrayed the fact that he was in some distress, yet spurred on by sheer guts and the will-to-win he scored the crucial winning goal. We still needed a positive result from our final match at Bournemouth but Strachan had undoubtedly ensured we had one foot firmly on the promotion ladder.

Just two years later, and aged 35 years and two months, Gordon was the captain of Leeds who stepped forward to collect the League Championship trophy. It must have been a moment of great pride for him and his family. My mind went back to our trip to Old Trafford eight months earlier when post-match interviews centred around the two skippers, Gordon and Bryan Robson. It was clear that within their very genuine and deep friendship there was still the rivalry to see which one of the old-timers could win the Champion's medal that had eluded them both during their illustrious careers.

It may have surprised some that Gordon emerged as the victor in that particular race. But make no mistake, Strachan has been good for Leeds, just as Leeds have been good for Strachan.

Chapter 4

ENGLAND MANAGER OR PRIME MINISTER?

'The chairman's wife consulted her astrological charts and said I was the man for the job.'

At times the suggestion that I was a future candidate for the job of managing the England national team was hung around my neck like a noose. Every utterance I have made about our national side, every move I've made in my career has been seen in some quarters as taking me inexorably towards the goal of one day managing England. The adherents of that particular theory must be unaware of the reasons why some people within the Football Association may never want me in charge of the national side. My detractors will invariably cite memories of an international snub that I knew at the time would linger long into the future.

There's also no doubt in my mind that international management in this country is blighted by difficulties that are virtually insurmountable. The England manager is simply set up to be shot down with no sense of realism or perspective applied by his critics, both within football and within the media. When you consider the increasing demands on players at club level the chances of producing a fresh, inventive side to tackle the cream of world football on an international stage are remote in the extreme. How can we allow a system that sees our best players forced to make 60 to 70 appearances in a long, hard season and then believe they can still turn it on when a collection of our individuals are put together for one-off games or a bi-annual tournament?

There is a delicious irony in the fact that Graham Taylor is the present incumbent, given the way our managerial careers have been inextricably linked for so long and that many years ago I was offered the chance of succeeding him by Lincoln City. As youngsters we had played against each other in English Grammar Schools' matches. Graham was a full-back with Lincolnshire while I was on the wing for Yorkshire. I eventually joined Sheffield Wednesday as a player while Graham went to Grimsby and then Lincoln where his career was cut short by injury.

We qualified as FA full badge coaches around the same time, were appointed FA staff coaches around the same time and were aked to staff national coaching courses around the same time. When Graham took control at Lincoln I was moving into management down the road with non-League Boston United. During our time in Lincolnshire we met as adversaries in the local county cup competitions as well as the FA Cup. When Graham moved to Watford many people would see the opportunity for me to take over at Sincil Bank as an ideal first step in League management.

I attended the interview at Lincoln on a Monday evening and it dragged on long into the night. I eventually arrived home in the early hours only to be woken a few hours later by a telephone call from the Lincoln Chairman, Mr Heanage Dove. He said he was offering me the job having spent all night discussing the situation with his wife, who was a great believer in astrology. Given the impression I had made at the interview and his wife's astrological predictions, based on the data available to her, he expressed, with the certainty of a zealot, that my appointment was the right move for Lincoln.

Many of my friends thought I was stupid to reject the Lincoln offer – perhaps success was mapped out for us in the stars. But given my age at the time and Lincoln's limited potential I felt it wasn't the right job for me. My view has always been that wherever I was working – be it Boston, Mossley, Notts County, Sheffield Wednesday or Leeds – I approached the job with the attitude that this would be my job for life. I can honestly say I have never had a strong ambition while I was in a job to look across to the greener pastures elsewhere with a view to moving on. As I frequently tell players, both young and old, in football we may have contracts but in many ways we're self-employed. The work we produce is the recommendation for the employement we will enjoy in the future.

The major blemish on my relationship with the FA came in October 1987 after Sheffield Wednesday had made a disastrous start to the season. The fact that the club had been hit by a crippling injury toll, with five senior players sidelined with fractures or serious injuries, counted for little as we slipped towards the foot of the First Division. The warning signs had been present from the previous Christmas when we failed to take the initiative to climb into second place and saw the season drift towards mid-table mediocrity.

Unfortunately, the plans I vociferously outlined that summer to revamp the club were not put into practice. We were stretching players to the limit and we had reached the point where the elastic was beginning to fray, and in some cases, snap. By mid-October there was only one team below us in the table. I had agreed to take charge of an England 'B' team that was travelling to Malta the following week when we were beaten 4-2 at Hillsborough by Manchester United.

I was well aware that in many people's eyes we were relegation material. After the United game I had a long chat with my number two Peter Eustace and vowed, somewhat emotionally and with much table-thumping, that if we were forced to throw apprentices into the fray we could survive on the organisation and team-work inherent within Sheffield Wednesday at that time. Nevertheless, a pearl of wisdom passed on to me by Jimmy Sirrel during our days together at Notts County, suddenly hit me between the eyes. Jimmy had observed the rocky ride Dave Sexton had suffered at Manchester United while remaining in control of the England Under-21 team. Jimmy pointed out that international commitments could become a potential Achilles heel for a manager and provide ammunition for his critics be they inside the boardroom, in the media or on the terraces. In the final analysis, the club paid the manager's wages so you owed your first allegiance to your club, over and above any personal considerations.

I had been weighing up the situation during the previous week before I recalled Jimmy's gem. Sadly, on that Saturday evening, and after much soul searching, I decided I would have to ask Bobby Robson to find someone else – if possible – to lead the trip to Malta. I realised it would have serious consequences regarding any prospect I had of working for the FA in the future. I had enjoyed many happy, worthwhile, educational years working for Ron Greenwood and Bobby Robson. I had steadily climbed the ladder and some people saw me as a possible heir apparent working for Bobby.

I telephoned Wednesday Chairman Bert McGee to inform him of my intention to pull out of the England commitment. I have to admit I did harbour the faint hope that he might somehow talk me out of my stance. This was not the time though to be leaving Wednesday. The England 'B' team were due to assemble the next day and I rang Bobby to ask to be excused. Bobby understood my dilemma and pointed out that in some respects my best plan might be to travel to Malta to get a break from the pressures of Hillsborough and allow the players a few days grace from me. The key issue though was the plight of Wednesday and I knew I had to stay in England to work with my team.

Bobby was very understanding. Ironically, it was Graham Taylor who answered England's SOS call and who knows the ramifications within the FA International Committee of my decision to miss the trip to Valetta?

Nobody in their right mind can go into football management with the clear-cut ambition of becoming England manager. I often draw the analogy with politics and the ludicrous notion that these days an overtly ambitious young man, or woman, might conspire to seek the nation's highest office. There are so many pitfalls along the way and good fortune is such a vital ingredient. The time span in climbing to the summit in politics, as in football, can prove far greater than a man's working life. The job only becomes available intermittently during the politician's career and your party may be in opposition when, in every other respect, you are the perfect man for the challenge ahead as prime minister. Unfortunately, the vacancy is tantalisingly only available to the other side. That's how I view the England football manager's job.

I went to work full-time for the FA after six happy years with Boston and six equally happy months with Mossley. One of my first tasks was to manage an England non-League representative side and this proved a great thrill and opportunity for me. I know there were mutterings inside Lancaster Gate about the thorough preparation that was involved in producing the team in proper shape for a two-game tournament which I'm proud to say we won. And it was success in this supposedly low-key event that led to my big break into League football.

It was also during my time with the FA that I was recruited by Ron Greenwood, then the England manager, to work as coach with the Under-21 side. I am indebted to Ron for introducing me to an area of football that has subsequently proved invaluable to my overall approach to management. Thanks to Ron I formed a priceless association with likes of Dave Sexton, Terry Venables, Bobby Robson and Don Howe. For just over ten years I spent time with the youth team, Under-21's, 'B' team and, on a couple of occasions, coached the senior squad. It was all invaluable experience.

Ron's enthusiasm for football is inextinguishable and when he became national team manager he called a summit meeting of his coaches and advisers at a secluded Cheshire hotel one Sunday morning. The guest list included Bobby Robson, Terry Venables, Dave Sexton, Graham Taylor, Bill Taylor, Howard Wilkinson and also the Nottingham Forest duo, Brian Clough and Peter Taylor. The official get-together was scheduled to begin at 10.30 a.m. and the likes of Bobby Robson had travelled north from Ipswich and Terry Venables from London to be in attendance. Ron was his usual bubbly self, his sparkling eyes displayed laughter lines at the corners as he chatted away merrily. We drank our morning coffee and munched our biscuits.

Ron became increasingly edgy though as he noticed the clock ticking towards the appointed hour and still Clough and Taylor were not present. There were a few whispered asides about their potential whereabouts while Ron, in his forgiving way, made a series of polite half-excuses for their lateness. By 10.45, though, even Ron had had enough. He decided we should start and led us to an ornate private room on the first floor of the old hotel.

Twenty-five minutes later, with a loud knock, the double doors burst open and Brian and Peter filled the doorway carrying what appeared to be an individual bottle of champagne for every guest and a glass each. Before anyone could speak Cloughie announced, 'Good morning gentlemen. I know you all think I'm an ignorant sod and just to prove it we've arrived late today but perhaps this champagne will ease the pain.'

He then went on to blame Taylor for their lateness, something Peter took in his half-embarrassed stride. Brian opened the bottles, poured drinks for everyone and then, with one final flourish, rolled his tracksuit trousers up to his knees before sinking into his chair.

When Bobby Robson succeeded Ron he offered me the chance to become his permanent number two. It was an invitation I turned down because I felt it was the right job at the wrong time for me. It would have been a mistake for me to go into full-time international management without achieving the success I was striving for in League football – at that time with Sheffield Wednesday. Thankfully, it proved to be the right decision. I still worked in an advisory capacity for Bobby, attending European Championship and World Cup finals to prepare reports on England's future opponents.

I put particular effort into an analysis of the Holland team that appeared in, and eventually won, the 1988 European Championships in Germany. After scrutinising them twice I headed for England's sumptuous hideaway hotel to inform Bobby of my views and a plan for the national side. We were scheduled to talk in the morning but that meeting was delayed and lunch was taken. In the afternoon a round of golf was suggested as a break for Bobby and coach Don Howe, so, with me in attendance, a party headed off down the fairway. Dinner had been served before I could deliver my blueprint for success against the Dutch masters, so finally, late in the evening, a three-hour talk-in began.

I praised the Dutch team for their inventive passing and their unselfish willingness to accept Ruud Gullit as the focal point of their movements. I suggested that England skipper Bryan Robson should be deployed in midfield to man-mark Gullit. That was a radical approach but one that I felt sure would also discomfort the captain of Holland and have the effect, through surprise, of knocking them out of their stride.

I suggested that when Holland were in possession every England player would have to adopt a man-marking role and force possession on to their defender Van Tiggelen. I argued that there was less danger with him in possession than the likes of Ronald Koeman and Frank Rijkaard. England would deploy Gary Lineker up-front with either John Barnes or Chris Waddle acting as a wide attacker. He would be fed the ball constantly and be told to run at his marker. If Barnes was deployed at the start he should be warned that a non-effective display would provoke his withdrawal and Waddle's introduction . . . or vice versa.

Don, in good devil's advocate fashion, did argue against the plan but after much debate the strategy was agreed. The team was set to prepare next day for the game and I looked forward to the match with real anticipation. Unfortunately, by the time Lineker and his mates were being informed the whole Wilkinson plan had been ditched. I gained no satisfaction as England were torn apart and lost 3-1. Before anyone suggests this is all anti-Robson sour grapes I must also point out that during the World Cup finals in Italy I was the man who told Bobby, 'You'll have no problems against Cameroon in the quarter-finals. It'll be a walk-over. It's as good as a bye.' So who am I to scrutinise the potential pitfalls of international management?

Inevitably, Leeds' Championship triumph focused international attention on my career and I received in the past close season a series of approaches from one particular club, desperate to persuade me to move abroad. I had no difficulty in turning down their initial inquiry about my availability and even agreed to their request to make Sheffield United manager Dave Bassett aware of their search for a coach. I tracked down Dave and his wife Christine, who are great family friends, dinner partners and neighbours in Sheffield, to their holiday villa in Portugal and, with profuse apologies for the intervention, asked whether he would fancy moving to the continent. Dave had agreed a new long-term contract with the Bramall Lane club before his departure and, as I had guessed, declined to pursue the matter.

I was ready to extend our joint apologies to the intermediary when I was told that the club in question had called a special board meeting the previous day and that they had decided I must be offered an 'open cheque' to persuade me to leave Leeds. The spending power to recruit top players was included in the ambitious policy and details of my contract were then delivered.

Galatasaray of Istanbul may not rank as one of Europe's premier clubs but they are one of Turkey's most established sporting institutions, with origins in the former British-run grammar school in the city renowned as the gateway to Asia. They suggested that by joining them for two years I would be guaranteed an income of around £1 million with all the benefits a move abroad – particularly from a taxation point of view – can provide. Galatasaray are also very pro-English, as epitomised by the names of some of their former coaches such as Don Howe, Malcolm Allison and Brian Birch. In fact, it was when Brian was in charge that they enjoyed a purple patch, winning three domestic titles on the trot.

It was Jack Charlton, my predecessor at Sheffield Wednesday and currently the team manager of the Republic of Ireland, who pointed out that financial independence gave great freedom to a manager: the freedom that allowed him to make decisions that may be unpopular but he knew were right and the security to walk away from a job when he realised the time for farewells had arrived. From that point of view the Galatasaray offer was attractive. As a coach the principle of working abroad, speaking a different language and working within a different culture, has always appealed to me. I believe that kind of challenge could be very stimulating.

But the time was not right for me to honestly give a second thought to anything beyond Leeds United and our plans for the coming European Cup campaign. My greatest ambition in management had also been two-fold. Initially, of course, it was to win a League title and then go on to lift Europe's most prestigious trophy – the European Champions' Cup. My summer's football work was planning for that particular odyssey.

The offer that gave me my big break in League football, to join Notts County, also came completely out of the blue. I drove to a deserted Meadow Lane on a hot July day and, before my appointment with Jimmy Sirrel, walked around the perimeter of the stadium. I then strolled around the inside of the ground, studying what could never be described as one of England's most attractive or best-equipped stadia. I knocked on the door to the old manager's office and was ushered by Jimmy into a neat and tidy cubby-hole in the dressing-room area of the ground.

Jimmy didn't waste time and told me he wanted me to become County's first-team coach. In fact, he was typically forthright as he made a confession to me. He said in that clipped, guttural, Glaswegian tongue, 'Lately son, I've found it more and more difficult to make the buggers run.' He expanded on that theme in his own, inimitable fashion, explaining how, if he could run, he would still be a foot-baller. As he was frequently fond of telling the County players, 'If you cannot run, you cannot play.'

I was very sceptical about the whole scenario. I had made enquiries before meeting Jimmy and was well aware of his reputation as the man who did everything. It was soccer legend that at Brentford and Aldershot Jimmy took charge of the laundry, the pitch, the treatment of injuries as well as picking the team. I told him I didn't see any point in me joining him on anything approaching that basis. He then vowed that if I took the job he would replace the tracksuit with a lounge suit, which he did immediately, albeit metaphorically. On that basis I agreed to become County's coach and with Jimmy, who is now the chief scout at Derby County, forged a relationship that has stood the test of time and is still as strong today.

Jimmy's waspish tongue could inflict serious damage and I agreed that after I had delivered the main team talk Jimmy would add his own personal addenda if he thought such was necessary. It goes without saying he always found it neces-sary. We used to take the County players to the National Watersports Centre at Holme Pierrepoint before matches.

The rooms were fairly spartan but the lads could rest and we would hold a team meeting there. On this particular occasion we were due to face Tommy Docherty's Queen's Park Rangers in a League Cup-tie and I casually mentioned to Jimmy that I wanted to have a quiet word with our main striker Trevor Christie who, I sensed, needed a little gee up.

Unfortunately, Jimmy's 'wee word' became a few wee words and then a few more until we were running behind schedule and forced to dash to Meadow Lane. In the dressing-room he asked me whether I'd spoken to Trevor and when I told him I hadn't had the chance he advised me to leave the matter to him. He asked Trevor into the medical room and declared, 'The manager wanted a word with you, son, but time has not been kind to us so I shall speak with you instead. Big fellow, you are an effing coward.'

My heart sank. I could see Trevor taking three months or more to get over this. I thought our chances were doomed and that I would face a major challenge in trying to rebuild a working relationship with a key player. Instead, Christie simply replied in his broad Geordie, 'I'll prove you wrong like.' To my total and utter surprise he went out, played like a hero and scored a goal as we defeated Rangers 4-1.

There's no doubt that the knowledge I built up during my time at Meadow Lane, working for Jimmy and Chairman Jack Dunnett, has been fundamental to me in my managerial career. As a bonus we also enjoyed many happy days together. I had joined Notts at Christmas-time and we had a battle to stay in the Second Division, but the following year we won promotion to the First Division and I enjoyed two relatively successful seasons in the top flight as County's team manager. My reputation appeared to be blossoming and I was offered the chance to become manager of West Bromwich Albion following a recommendation from Ron Greenwood.

Albion's Chairman at that time was Bert Millichip, also chairman of the FA, and he had sought advice from Ron about a new manager. The Hawthorns job did have its attractions. Albion had enjoyed some successful times, particularly when Ron Atkinson was in charge, and I realised the contract offered by them was better than anything I could ever expect at little old Notts. But I sensed that my next move had to be to a club that offered me the chance to compete with the very best in the country. I believed if I continued to work hard and produce a relatively successful County team the right offer would one day come along. I just had to keep up the good work at Meadow Lane. Fortunately, time was to prove that decision correct.

If Sheffield Wednesday had been 24 hours later in offering me their manager's job, Jack Dunnett would have had me tied to County on a new long term contract. But Dunnett, formerly a Labour MP, and wealthy businessman who served in office as president of the Football League, was famed for his protracted negotiations. He loved being locked in talks and, true to form, his opening offer to me was way below what we both knew I merited. Over a period of days we edged closer until, just before the contract was signed and sealed, Wednesday appeared on the horizon.

Jack Charlton had been in charge at Hillsborough for six very successful years. He had taken them from the brink of bankruptcy and life in the Third Division to the upper reaches of Division Two. But to Jack's frustration he had failed in his ambition of guiding them back into the top flight. I thought about Wednesday's proposition and decided, like Leeds in 1988, they had the genuine potential to compete with the best, providing the people in control agreed with my strong views on how their rich potential might be maximised to secure a place in football's big six.

There was no doubt then, or now, in my mind about Wednesday's capabilities. That conviction was merely confirmed when we finished fifth in the First Division in 1986 and would have qualified for the UEFA Cup but for the ban imposed on English clubs following the Heysel Stadium disaster. It was also confirmed last season when, under Trevor Francis's astute management, they finished third and did enjoy the rewards of a place in Europe.

It was during that particularly successful period at Hillsborough that two offers from abroad came my way which, in many respects, would have dramatically altered my life. I was given permission by Wednesday Chairman Bert McGee to meet a representative of Saudi Arabian club Aitihad. I recall the meeting at a Hertfordshire hotel the night before a match in London. I met a suave Arab gentleman who spent six months working in London as Chairman of an investment corporation and the rest of the year in the Middle East. The financial package he detailed was astonishing.

Over three years I was guaranteed £500,000 net with the potential to double that amount through bonuses if the team was successful. I would also be given the best investment advice and analyses. Aitihad believed this was an offer I couldn't refuse – after all, I was *en route* to becoming a millionaire with the prospect of having my financial future secured for life. As far as I was concerned though the Saudi deal was a total non-starter. Money is not everything and I had ambitions to fulfil, dreams of attaining success in English football that were precious to me. I also rejected a lucrative offer from Greek club PAOK Salonika for exactly the same reasons.

A strange job offer, out of the blue, that came to me during my time at Hillsborough was a post that Bobby Robson assured me was the very best in English club football. It was the opportunity to become manager of Bobby's former club, Ipswich Town. Patrick Cobbold, the old Ipswich Chairman, telephoned me while on a fishing holiday in Scotland. The offer was attractive and the Cobbold family had a deserved reputation within the game for allowing their managers to get on with running the club without undue hindrance. I was very tempted. The whole set-up, and the idea of living in East Anglia was very appealing. However, I calculated, rightly or wrongly, that my next management stint should be, if possible, with a club that could compete financially with the big boys. So I had to offer Ipswich a somewhat reluctant 'No, thank you.'

Chapter 5

THE SLIPPERY SLOPE

'The cheap coaches are the first to get sacked.'

Brian Clough has always maintained the 44 days he spent at Leeds made him the great manager he has become over the past 20 years. The compensation he received after being sacked by Leeds, believed to be in the region of £98,000, which in 1973 was not an inconsiderable sum, completely transformed Cloughie's approach to his professional duties. Before the day Leeds sacked him he perhaps felt he made decisions without security. From that fateful day on he faced every challenge secure in the knowledge he could do whatever he thought was right for his club and himself. He need pay lip service to no man.

Managers have to pay the bills and even though there are ex-players who have secured themselves financially forever and a day through their lucrative playing careers, they still tend to be the exceptions. The work-a-day manager is still very much a vital part of football.

Johan Cruyff once asserted, 'The cheap coaches are the first to get sacked', and that philosophy still rings true although with an annual salary of some £1.2 million the Barcelona coach is well insulated against any professional mishaps. People persistently ask me what it's like to be a manager and I always used to be reluctant to answer. I felt mine might be an individual view that was not easily accepted by my managerial counterparts. Since I've become the inaugural Chairman of the League Managers' Association part of my responsibilities has been to talk to other managers in a wider sense than just our day-to-day involvement in the game. The public perception of managers as highly paid, high-living superstars would be destroyed forever if they only knew the kind of salaries many members of the LMA receive and the hassles they face in getting their rightful compensation payments when they are prematurely dismissed.

I now realise my observations on management are echoed in many quarters and I often see our job as very similar to that of the mountaineers in the Edwardian era when, for the wealthy, fulfilling the grand tour of Europe was the done thing. Climbing the mountains with very limited equipment was an immense challenge and, recognising this, many spectators were attracted to avidly scrutinise the mountaineers' every move from adjacent vantage points. Those were the days of real rope, converted walking shoes and bundles of bravery.

Watching the climbers was indeed a very popular spectator sport. The men would inch their way up the Eiger using primitive equipment, well aware of the danger below but galvanised into action by their pursuit of glory. A season in League management is very similar. We all start together at the foot of the mountain and we think we possess basically the same equipment. Like the mountaineer, the manager believes he knows the strategy that will eventually out-flank the rivals alongside him as they climb the perilous rock face. But it quickly becomes very clear that some are better prepared than others.

It's not just down to equipment and tactics but also elusive qualities like good luck and weather conditions. Suddenly, there are casualties and we become aware that the casualties are attractive to the on-lookers. The spectators are peering down their telescopes to pick out the first sign of distress. Every detail is magnified in their world just as for the manager the media often focus on his potential demise.

The men who fell off the mountain were sometimes applauded for their courage or lambasted for their stupidity. The failed manager is treated in a similar manner. People fall off the football mountain to the extent that last season, of the 93 League clubs involved at the outset, well over one-third lost their manager. Like the climbers we know the risks but it's still difficult at times to quite forgive and forget the lack of insight shown by those who are supposed to know better.

Survival is a basic instinct in all of us – managers are no different. You can't get away from that. It's a fundamental tenet of football. I constantly emphasise to my players the business of surviving out on that pitch, that once they cross the white line they shouldn't be passengers and shouldn't expect help. Firstly, they must aim to survive and if they achieve that objective they can start helping others. But it's difficult to win a football match if three of four of your team are losing their personal battles with their immediate opponents.

In a football club the battle for survival predominates, not just on a match day, but all week. Inside a dressing-room a definite pecking order develops as players recognise their place, whether it be linked to a social or entertainment order. It's well known for players to survive at a club because of their ability to manipulate people, especially team-mates, when on sheer ability alone they should have been exposed as impostors.

This ebb and flow of human emotion provides the backdrop as the manager manages to succeed or succeeds to manage!

I was delighted to accept an invitation in May 1992 to attend a special coaching convention at the Italian FA's training camp Corverciano, near Florence. The coaches/managers of the five Champion clubs from Italy, Germany,

Holland, France and England were brought together to share their experiences in front of an audience of Italian coaches. There was a prize to be awarded to the outstanding coach, called the 'Panchina d'oro', which literally translates as the 'Golden Bench'. I don't think any of the four visitors to Italy was surprised when AC Milan's Fabio Capello won the accolade. It was a fitting, and predictable, finale to his club's remarkable achievement in remaining unbeaten throughout the entire Italian League campaign.

I was honoured to be named as a runner-up to Fabio and found it a pleasant challenge to detail not only how Leeds had won the English League but my own precepts of management. In certain respects, I suppose I was reviewing my own check list of what I saw as the important benchmarks of my job. Undoubtedly, the most critical aspect is preparation. The close season and pre-season are the times when you can do your most important work. Those who fail to prepare should be prepared to fail.

Professional players are like grand prix cars. The team manager at Ferrari will try to sign the best driver, but the company must give him the best car, the best mechanical back-up and the most astute analysis of the data relating to that priceless machine. Players must realise that their bodies are racing cars – the vehicles which will carry them to success.

Organisation should not limit or restrict a team's performance. By preparing properly you can remove the doubt and uncertainty from as many minds as possible. The coach must ascertain all the scenarios within a football match that can be predicted and help his players deal with these. This leaves the players' minds free to concentrate on the unpredictable and to produce their own moments of ingenuity and expression.

For instance, set-pieces can be crucial because 50 per cent of goals come from them. During our Championship season we reached December before we conceded a goal from a corner. It was January before we conceded a goal from a free-kick which required a wall of three or more players. I don't want to sound like a Treasury spokesman trying to blind people with statistics but the merits of this kind of approach are undoubtedly worthwhile.

I recall signing for Sheffield Wednesday an ageing centre-back from Nottingham Forest called Paul Hart. Harty was an experienced pro who had served Forest, Leeds, Blackpool and Stockport well. But he told me he had never been asked to spend the time on the training ground perfecting set-piece drills that we invested at Wednesday. He admitted he was sceptical about the issue. Paul was used as a very adept target for our long throw-ins and in-swinging corners. Fortunately, we put together a run where we scored 13 goals in 14 con-secutive games with set-plays. Consequently, he was forced to review his objections. He became a convert.

In fairness to Paul, when he had a go at management with Chesterfield, he happily invested similar time in set-piece practices and, as a result, enjoyed some rewards for his ideas and endeavours.

One of the great problems for any tactician in England is coping with the variety of styles utilised by the opposition. Cheap jokes abound. The ball may need painkillers after a Wimbledon game. It may fall asleep in some Nottingham Forest matches. You have to learn how to deal with the ostensibly long-ball teams, then the following week, you are asked to combat Forest who want to play the ball to feet and utilise the skills of Nigel Clough in his deep-lying striker role.

It's not just style that alters from week to week either, but basic formations. On the continent the norm is to use a sweeper whereas in England we predominantly prefer a flat back four but sweepers still pop up and so your strikers have to be instructed in how to combat the extra man at the back. Again, I prefer the idea of working out two or three distinct strategies with my players to cover each eventuality before a ball is kicked in the coming season. This kind of collective team thinking is as vital a part of their preparation as their fitness work. When the need arises they can more easily switch into a mode we have worked on together.

A manager must be able to set his players realistic goals. Motivation is not just a quarter to three thing on a Saturday afternoon when the crowd are piling into the ground and anticipation buzzes around the dressing-room. Motivation, if it is to be effective, is for life. That's one of the reasons why at Leeds the idea of two contracts is very important. The first is the traditional written agreement, lodged with the League and covering wages and bonuses. The second contract is unwritten but, to my mind, infinitely more important. This is where the players decide and say what they want to achieve. This personal commitment is crucial. It is their personal testament, a sort of moral pledge about which the screw can be turned if necessary.

Real confidence, the self-belief that matters most, comes from ability. Talent gives you the potential to answer any of those questions which might be posed out on the football field. However, as with the golfer, if you only have three clubs in your bag you can only play so many shots. If you have 15 clubs in your bag you have the potential to play many more shots. It is also important to recognise that you have five times the potential to make mistakes.

Players have to realise that talent on its own is not enough. It has to be directed. The top-class athlete recognises his life in sport is about winning. Some people play to play, successful people play to win. For the coach, or manager, talent can broaden his horizons. Talent determines what he can do with his players and how he can do it. Like the artist, the talent of his players decides the scope, depth and breadth of the picture the coach can paint.

It used to annoy me when I was striving to get Wednesday recognised as one of the clubs in football's élite that continual comparisons would be made between my lads and Liverpool. We were always being reminded that we weren't as good as the Merseysiders but were still challenged to produce the kind of entertainment and flowing soccer expected of that footballing institution. Our critics overlooked the fact that in their formative days under Bill Shankly and the early Bob Paisley period Liverpool travelled away from home and camped out defensively to clinch a boring goal-less draw at places like Derby and Leeds. Those great managers had realistic aims for the teams and prepared them accordingly. It was only when Liverpool accumulated more and more outstanding players that they could play a more expansive game and eventually dominate any opponents.

Send out an average team to copy the Liverpool method and you'll end up with average results. It can't be done like that. It takes years of success to build the platform which dictates the way you're going to play and that can only be achieved by eventually producing or attracting great players to a club weaned on success.

I know Shankly and Paisley were both total pragmatists in tactical terms. I'm sure they would be in agreement with Barcelona coach Johan Cruyff's dictate. Cruyff may have been one of the great artists in world football during the past 30 years and he still encourages his team to attack at every opportunity, but as he asserted before the European Cup final against Sampdoria at Wembley, 'I would rather win a poor match than lose a good one.'

The kind of harrowing lesson experienced by Mike Smith, a fine international manager, when he took charge of Hull City should not be forgotten. Mike, who had enjoyed great success as Wales manager, took with him to Boothferry Park more proven coaches than a club of Hull's status could probably justify. He set about his task in an impeccable manner and when I visited him on a match day I was impressed by his office with all its charts and diagrams which no doubt had the right theoretical basis.

I asked Mike how he was faring and he said he'd virtually sifted through the playing staff. 'Another couple out of the door and I'll have a good ship with a very honest crew,' he said. I recall pointing out to Mike that if Hull didn't start winning games quickly the directors might lose interest in his crew-cleansing initiative and he might find himself out of work.

Mike scratched his head and felt I was being over-cynical. He had thoroughly discussed with his directors how the club should be run. They were all sensible, rational people, successful in their own businesses, and Mike felt secure in the knowledge that their views and commitment mirrored his. I took no pleasure in seeing it happen but soon afterwards Mike was relieved of his duties. Management can be so very difficult and so very disappointing.

Successful results are imperative and inevitably encourage a realistic approach. It's almost equally inevitable though that some managers will opt for the world of football fantasy, where style and quality become of paramount importance. Since being thrashed 6-3 at Wembley by Hungary in 1953 it has been a problem for us in England to understand and decide what constitutes good football. As different teams have become successful so our ideas seem to change. No team has dominated world soccer to the extent that their approach effectively wipes out all other arguments.

During my managerial career I've been publicly vilified as a high priest of long-ball football, thanks to my early days at Sheffield Wednesday. Leeds also came in for some 'route one' abuse but that, to a degree, was a concomitant part of life with Leeds, the most hated club in English football. My detractors seem to overlook the fact that Notts County were a passing team to the extent that if we didn't have 34 touches before we crossed the half-way line we would knock the ball back to the goalie to start again.

At Leeds our style has evolved with the recruitment of better players and the same approach was, to a lesser extent, true at Hillsborough. Every manager in the world is searching for football effectiveness. And believe it or not, the principles for winning a match in Italy or Uruguay are the same as in England, France or Cameroon. Obviously, things like climate, culture and the nature of competition affects things but we can also recognise certain differing approaches.

Look at the likes of Brazil, Italy and Spain. These are countries where the framework of football is based on pass and move techniques and where the ball is passed to feet. They search for the opportunity to reach those positions of great strategic importance by keeping relatively safe possession. They are happy to utilise six or seven passes if necessary.

At the other end of the spectrum you supposedly have the long-ball game. Undoubtedly, it can be effective and having viewed football all over the world it never ceases to amaze me that when a team that has been painstakingly building attacks for 70 minutes suddenly falls behind, the danger of defeat prompts a style of more direct, long-ball football. The goalie who wouldn't kick the ball at all suddenly launches it downfield on the basis that if the ball is near the opposition goal his team might get possession and score. Basically, all teams should be attempting to achieve the same things, and one of the most important of these is getting the ball into areas from which goals can be scored.

Instead of dissecting tactics I think there is more to be gained by looking at the quality of players. The world's great players are the models for how the game can be played. I would cite a quartet including George Best, Pele, Bobby Charlton and Franz Beckenbauer. Those players are adept at many things but, in particular, passing and controlling the ball. Consequently, they had no fear of receiving possession in any situation. And for many years I've wondered if the best test for a so-called world-class player is to ask whether he could operate anywhere on the field of play.

I think when you look at that quartet they could. I would have no hesitation in deploying Best as a centre-half. I'm sure he had the natural talent to do that job. But when you get in a competitive environment where results govern your survival you must look at ways of producing a style that works for your team and also limits the effectiveness of the opposition.

In my opinion, the true test of a coach and, unfortunately, I'm disappointed at the general standards football sets for its coaches, is to produce a team capable of displaying any type of football. Given time for preparation and the chance to assess the opposition's strengths he must work out ways to deal with them and make sure his own team can come good.

I always remind the players at Leeds not to start moaning about the so-called 'lack of quality' of our opponents' football. That sort of comment is worthless. If opponents are so poor they should be easy to beat. I firmly believe that if you want to prove the way you do things is best, then you prove it out on the pitch.

It is impossible though to keep every player within your club happy. The physical demands of the modern game have enforced the need for squads of strength and depth. But the kind of insurance the manager wants against a potential injury crisis inevitably leaves some players, who have tasted first-team action, kicking their heels in the reserves. Every player is realistic enough to recognise this potential scenario but, in the long run, the reality still proves unacceptable to many of them.

Noel Blake had been brought to Leeds by my predecessor Billy Bremner but during my time lost his first-team berth. Noel is a big lad who has muscles in his spit and when he flashes those menacing eyes you don't argue. He was disheartened about his prospects at Elland Road and asked my assistant Michael Hennigan to arrange a meeting with me. Michael popped in after training to relay Noel's request and I asked for 45 minutes grace while I fulfilled a prior arrangement. By 2.15 p.m. though I would be free so I sent Michael to the players' lounge to confirm the arrangements.

'Blakey, it's sorted out for you,' Michael announced. 'I've got you an audience with the gaffer at a quarter past two.'

'I don't want an audience,' came Noel's reply. 'I want to see him on my own.'

There are also testing times for managers and coaches in terms of relationships with players and the imposition of discipline within the club. I joined Notts County at Christmas time and recall my first night away with the team was on New Year's Eve before a home game against Cambridge. I was very much the new boy in the camp and when I heard a racket down the corridor from my bedroom at about 12.30 a.m. decided to tell the revellers to calm down because there were professional footballers trying to sleep in adjacent bedrooms.

I hammered on the door which opened to reveal nine County players enjoying their first drinks of the New Year and generally having a good time. It would be wrong to say they were tearing the place apart but I sensed all eyes in the room were on me, waiting to observe my reaction. They might have been pleased by my opening gambit, 'Have you got a glass for me, lads, before we have a little chat?'

I then expressed my extreme displeasure at their behaviour, their failure to accept a code of conduct expected of top sportsmen and suggested they head straight to their beds. Manager Jimmy Sirrel was on the floor below and unaware of the disturbance. I told the players I would not be running to inform the club or to demand fines. But, in my eyes, they were all now on trial and must never let me or County down again.

There may have been a temptation to try to win the players over by being their mate and turning a blind eye. I knew that was wrong and that a dividing line had to be drawn. I've stood by that principle of management ever since. Scrutinising the conduct of players and officials when a new manager takes over is always a fascinating affair and there was a comical moment on the return journey from Ipswich that marked Leeds' first away win under my control.

My car had been driven to Portman Road but I wanted to travel north on the team coach to have a chat with a few of the players and generally savour the taste of success with my new team. Physiotherapist Alan Sutton was deputed to drive my vehicle to a pre-arranged meeting place at the motorway services where he would fill it with petrol before I took over for the final leg to my home.

The team coach pulled alongside Alan as he stood replenishing the empty tank. But instead of using lead-free petrol he was filling it with diesel. The manager was not impressed. We had to leave the car there for the tank to be drained and I vowed not to make Alan my chauffeur again. He did survive the misdemeanour though.

Inevitably, given the spotlight employed by the media, it is the managers of the famous clubs who invariably hog the headlines. But, within the game, there have always been unsung heroes, saluted by their contemporaries and recognised as men of real ability who may not have landed one of the glamour jobs but still deserve total respect for their achievements.

Sadly, there are times when you think you've found an unsung hero of management only for his club to decide the man is dispensable. At a stroke they ditch him and he's out of work. Jimmy Sirrel told me during my early days with him at Notts County, 'There's only one thing certain for the likes of us and that's the sack.'

Jimmy wasn't a cynic. Even now, as chief scout at Derby County, he retains his boyish enthusiasm. Undoubtedly, Jimmy marched along the heroes' path, steadfastly avoiding the ambushes, the barbed wire and the flying grenades. But even he became a managerial casualty at Sheffield United. He was cleverly resuscitated by a very shrewd field surgeon in the shape of Notts County Chairman Jack Dunnett.

The League Managers' Association, through the good offices of Barclays Bank – a company which has, in my opinion, proved a true friend to football in recent years – instituted in May 1992 a new award at the annual 'Manager of the Year' luncheon. As well as honouring the men whose teams had invariably won the Divisional Championships, it was decided that all the management members should vote for their choice of man with rich managerial skills, whose team may not have won a trophy but who deserved recognition from his peers.

The inaugural winner was Dave Bassett of Sheffield United. 'Harry', as he's known throughout football, is a good friend of mine and he was a deserving recipient. His team finished ninth in the First Division on fewer resources than most and having stared relegation in the face around Christmas time. By the end of the campaign though, Sheffield United had survived, with something to spare. Realistically, what more could anyone ask? Will that be enough though, next year, or the year after that? I fear not.

When Harry took over at Bramall Lane, United were facing relegation from Division Two and he warned them they were beyond hope. He was proved right and had to launch his rebuilding plans from the Third Division. The progress from there has been remarkable. But keeping a realistic perspective when dealing with future events does not come easy to many connected with the game. Professional football is played for the players and the spectators. One way or another, the supporters, be they standing on the Kop or sat in an executive box, generate the interest and the finances which provide the life blood of the professional game.

In all good faith, the guardians of the clubs will claim to a man, as they relax in the warm summer sunshine, that their view is a sensible, dispassionate, realistic opinion. Unfortunately, when the same men are twitching and nervous by January a cold panic sets in and boardrooms become the setting for majority votes of no-confidence.

Perhaps the whole nature of management is now unfair because the demands for change seem to increase by the season. The sacked manager is seen as a minor casualty in order that football can continue as part of the entertainment industry. Even the good managers can become victims of their own ability. Having achieved success, or real progress, on a shoestring budget, why can't they perform even greater miracles the following year? There are other times when the manager can become intoxicated by his achievements and convince himself that, despite the mounting evidence to the contrary, he is the man who can break the mould.

So, who have been the heroes and where are today's crop? The inimitable Colin Murphy created a kingdom for himself at Lincoln City and would admit that he has entertained the football world with his very own brand of football prose. He's back in business at Southend so we will have to chart his progress with interest.

I'm sure Dario Gradi, the manager of Crewe Alexandra since 1983, has proved that, providing everyone adopts a sensible and fair approach, the team boss can attempt to launch long-term plans – even if his club are involved in a roller-coaster of promotion and relegation from season to season. In the period since the Second World War the average tenancy for a manager at Gresty Road was two years – if he was lucky. Dario has forced them to change that 'hire and fire' mentality.

Crewe haven't wanted to lose their manager just as Dario, whenever opportunities to move on have cropped up, has preferred to stick with them. From being a music hall joke club, Gresty Road is now on the essential list of venues for First Division managers and scouts to check for budding talent. Rob Jones' progress at Liverpool following his £300,000 transfer provided recent evidence of the Gradi academy. I sense that the greatest tribute Crewe can pay Gradi is that they do really appreciate the achievements he has brought their way, greater success than perhaps they have ever had the right to expect.

Living with a set-back, and treating with respect the man who has proved a worthy tactician in the past, was obviously a challenge for Port Vale last May when they were relegated from Division Two. John Rudge has spent nine years in charge at Vale Park and I trust all those people disappointed by the loss of Second Division status remembered the state of the club, then wallowing in Division Four, when Rudgey took over.

Arthur Cox tends not to sing his own praises so it's understandable that his acts of heroism have so often remained unsung. However, when you look at his track record, remembering he's been in charge of all sorts of clubs in all sorts of circumstances, Arthur is an outstanding manager. The advice one particular chairman kept proffering Arthur was, 'Tighten your belt. There's no money to spend.' Thankfully, he survived the demise of Robert Maxwell and Lionel Pickering's take-over at Derby County appears to have made Arthur's belt one of the slackest in the business. I understand the late Mr Maxwell often used nautical analogies relative to the running of his football clubs. It's probably appropriate then to view Arthur's departure from Newcastle in a similar vein. Captain Arthur was the wily old sea dog who had the judgment and intuition to escape the heady euphoria of St James's Park following a promotion triumph in 1984. He spotted the storm clouds brewing and found himself another ship down at Derby. Captain Bob just went overboard.

You don't need to be a genius to pick out the so-called sleeping giants in English football, the clubs that are desperate to be revived and guided to great glory again. Sadly, in some of the cases, the damage inflicted in the past is irreparable. Graham Turner, the manager of Wolverhampton Wanderers, is a man who has strenuously battled against the odds to get things right. Perhaps I'm not giving him the credit he deserves but I do praise Graham for his sensible assessment of the job he faces at Molineux and a large part of his success there relates to the hurdles he has had to overcome. You must choose the battles you think you can win if you want to win the war.

I think many of my contemporary managers were bitterly disappointed a few years ago when Huddersfield Town sacked their long-serving manager Mick Buxton. Mick may not have been a household name but his reputation inside football was unquestionable. In eight years as Huddersfield's manager he had lifted them from the foot of the Fourth Division and established them in the upper reaches of Division Two.

Under Mick's management Huddersfield could give any team a real challenge. His team was fast, direct and fit, a reflection of the highly competitive, yet honest, way Mick believed the game should be played. The football historians analysing his demise will cite a disappointing run of results and, that curse of so many managers, major changes in the boardroom. Suffice to say that six years on, and four managers later, Huddersfield have still not regained the status enjoyed during Mick's reign.

It would be interesting if a manager could insure himself against accident in much the same way as a driver of a car. Some managers might only get cover for third party, fire and theft. Some might be uninsurable. The football clubs and the directors that employ them would also have to be rated in categories like vehicles. For certain, there are one or two clubs in the limousine class with all the best, high-technology safety equipment fitted. There are also a few clubs with the sports roadster mentality, ready to cut a few corners in their bid to get to their destination in a hurry. I wonder how many clubs would be branded as unsafe and not roadworthy, unsuitable for use by any manager?

I can't see much changing in the immediate future either. The demise of Maidstone and Aldershot should not be viewed as exceptions. More and more clubs are going to have to come to terms with reality and decide what they have the right to expect. I know a young manager at the moment whose wage bill for his entire playing staff is £3,500 a week. That's right, about the same figure as some individual First

Division players receive. There are part-time clubs in non-League football paying more and doing quite nicely.

Life in the non-League world can provide a good grounding for managers and administrators. For instance, Alan Hardy was club secretary when I was with Mossley and he's now commercial manager at Oldham Athletic. Barry Fry has adjusted to life in the Football League with Barnet, just as Neil Warnock brought Scarborough out of the Conference and eventually moved on to Notts County.

A band of young managers who were rivals during my days with Boston have proved their worth. Ron Atkinson was in charge at Kettering in those days, David Pleat was at Nuneaton Borough and I was initially player-coach for Jim Smith at Boston United. I think it was Ron who suggested that managers should adopt the suitably heroic motto originally inspired by the gladiators in Rome. 'Moriture te salutant', which means, 'Those about to die salute you.' Perhaps we should have the motto engraved and hung over every manager's door.

Chapter 6

THE TAINTED TASTE
OF PROMOTION

*'Leeds had become the most hated club in football. Earning
the right to be respected as a caring club with discipline
instilled at its core was a paramount objective.'*

The champagne flowed in the cramped dressing-room that
was more like a sauna on that swelteringly hot Saturday in
May. Players, famed within the game for their physical
bravery, toughness and, at times, their cynicism, wept
openly. Leeds were back in the First Division after an eight-
year exile, but our moment of triumph had been grievously
marred by the scenes of violence around Dean Court and in
Bournemouth on that sunny weekend.

The potential for debate about the exact reasons for the
appalling events in the Hampshire resort remains immense. I
believe unequivocally that the Bournemouth-Leeds fixture
should not have taken place on that particular day – a Bank
Holiday weekend that coincided with the frantic climax to
the League season. We can retrace all the old ground about
how many fans from other clubs arrived in Bournemouth on
that weekend hoping for confrontations with the thousands
of Leeds followers in town. We can also question the wisdom
of the many ticketless supporters who ignored pleas to stay
away from the tiny home stadium of AFC Bournemouth.

I cannot, and would never, attempt to excuse the people

supposedly connected with Leeds United who behaved so shamefully during that weekend. I made it clear at the time, and willingly repeat now, that we do not want any of those individuals to follow our club. They only bring shame on us and supporters all over England. Sadly, the stigma attached to Leeds United rears its ugly head whenever there is the slightest semblance of crowd disorder. Let's be frank. Over a number of years Leeds became the most hated institution in football. Earning the right to be respected with a new reputation as a caring club, a club with discipline instilled at its core and possessing a team that produced attractive football were among my paramount objectives when I took over in 1988.

One of the saddest aspects about the events in Bournemouth was that until that juncture we had been winning the battle to improve our public relations image. Every player at Elland Road during my time in charge has been repeatedly counselled about the high standards of discipline expected of him. Some found that self-control hard to maintain. They tended to be the players quickly shown the door. For instance, in a pre-season friendly against Anderlecht one of our players chose to punch an opponent in the face. His action was both uncalled for and totally inexplicable. I'm sure the referee, who was only yards away from the incident, could hardly believe his eyes. Even worse, on the eve of the new season the player had stupidly earned himself a three-match ban. It was ill-discipline bordering on soccer suicide.

I recognised when I accepted the challenge of managing Leeds that ridding the club of its old, unsavoury image might prove beyond me, my players and the directors at the club. But cut through the prejudice and the hype and I think we have travelled a long way down the road to success on that particular issue. You can become paranoid about media criticism. In the main, and I have to admit here that I did object to some of the reporting and suggestions of sanctions in the immediate aftermath of Dean Court, I believe in recent times we have received fair and just Press coverage. I think the knowledgeable writers have recognised the genuine, wholehearted attempts that have been made to get things right.

During the past three seasons the crowd behaviour of Leeds fans inside and outside stadia has improved. The slightest deterioration, though, inevitably brings its welter of 'notorious fans' stories. Sadly, the situation following the Bournemouth match was all too predictable. Leeds, not for the first time, were the recipients of the kind of media abuse no other club has suffered. Some of the proposed punishments went beyond anything any court in this land would perceive as justice. Would we be promoted? Would Elland Road be closed? Should we be forced to play away games behind closed doors?

Eventually, when the dense fog of irrationality had cleared away, we were accepted as Second Division Champions. I can now reflect on the events of that weekend with a mixture of pleasure at getting so many aspects of the adventure right and bitter disappointment that the club's reputation was yet again blighted in such an unwanted fashion.

We were locked in a three-way promotion battle with Sheffield United and Newcastle United. We were well aware that victory would guarantee us the Division Two title but that anything less might have us praying for good news from Sheffield's match at Leicester and Newcastle's north-east derby at Middlesbrough. I arranged to have scouts at both venues armed with mobile telephones who duly relayed information of the matches to Peter Ridsdale, one of our directors, at Bournemouth. I did this just in case there was a need to change our tactical approach or to make a substitution relative to results elsewhere.

In an attempt to escape the growing mood of expectancy around Yorkshire we opted to take the players to a New Forest hideaway on the Thursday. I tried to gear everything in training to be light-hearted and humorous and, apart from an unfortunate injury to midfielder Andy Williams, that plan had worked to perfection. Predictably, Vinnie Jones was involved in the training ground accident that saw Andy whisked to hospital. We had been playing a lot of non-stop cricket and baseball. Vinnie had smashed the ball into orbit and let go of the bat only to see it arc through the air and crash into Andy's face, resulting in him suffering a depressed cheek fracture.

That apart, everyone's spirits were high and on the Thursday night, for the first time in my reign at Leeds, we took all the players to dine together at an Italian restaurant. Sat around the table were virtually all the people, players and staff, who had contributed to our promotion campaign. The players were told they could have whatever they wanted to eat and, to a degree, whatever they wanted to drink. The team hotel was walking distance away so they could stay as long as they wanted. We deliberately delayed pre-match training until the Friday afternoon to allow the lads a leisurely morning. I had no fears of anybody abusing the hospitality. The preceding season had shown what a responsible bunch of players I'd had the privilege of working with. I knew they would respect the little extra freedom prior to such an important match.

Everyone was aware, even at this stage, that Bournemouth and its environs was packed with Leeds fans. The feeling grew among us that the authorities had got it wrong in insisting that this particular fixture had to go ahead. But the overall mood within the team was of quiet determination. I sensed there was no chance of us blowing our opportunity now. In effect, we dominated the game. We missed a string of chances and were frustrated to see their keeper Gerry Peyton pull off some fine saves but in the second half we made the all-important breakthrough. Chris Kamara, the veteran midfielder who had made such a telling contribution to our promotion challenge, burst down the right and clipped over an inviting cross. Lee Chapman rose to despatch a header of such power that it appeared to fly through Peyton's clutches.

The fact that Dave Bassett's Sheffield side had swamped Leicester 5-2 and that Newcastle had been defeated 4-1 at Ayresome Park was suddenly immaterial. We were unassailable Champions. In footballing terms everything we had set out to achieve in phase one of the re-birth of Leeds had been achieved. The lads prepared for a long and boisterous trip back to Yorkshire after the match but I stayed with my family at a friend's home in the New Forest. We enjoyed a terrific meal on the Saturday night, made even better by some superb wine. I rose early the next day and sat by the outdoor swimming pool, listening to the dawn chorus. Everything was perfect, an exquisite antidote to the draining year's work I had put in and the unwanted excesses of the previous day. I knew from my Hillsborough experience how physically and emotionally shattering a promotion campaign can be. I vowed never to allow football to take that sort of toll on me again. I have a photograph at home which captures the celebratory hugs Peter Eustace, Alan Smith and I shared on Sheffield Wednesday's promotion. Promoted? I looked as if I'd just come out of a prison camp. My friend John Mills' garden, with the birds in celebratory song, was the ideal place to be.

Winning the Second Division was always going to be a mammoth task. We had made our intentions clear by investing in the likes of Gordon Strachan, Chris Fairclough and Vinnie Jones. We were accused in a simplistic manner of trying to buy promotion but this was far from the truth. You can buy players but you can't buy points. The player recruitment was part of a much longer term project and in real cash terms our investment had not been that remarkable, especially when you consider the spending of clubs outside the top flight these days. We still faced the flak though.

After we had played out a 1-1 draw with Blackburn Rovers at Elland Road in our third game of the season I bumped into the late Bill Fox, Rovers' Chairman and President of the Football League, and his manager Donald Mackay. They were striding, heads high, down the main staircase, looking more than a little pleased with themselves, as indeed they had the right to. Bill pointed out, 'Wilki, management's not about all these big transfers you're involved in. A good manager should be picking up bargain buys and making something of them. Managing without brass. That's the measure of a manager.'

I looked Bill and Donald in the eye and calmly explained, 'I've done it your way, now I'm doing it my way and I know which I prefer. Let's discuss it again next May, shall we?'

The fact that we were odds-on favourites to win promotion just pumped up the expectation level even more but I felt the key factor was to recognise the very specific demands of coping with a 46-game season against such varied opponents. There would be the high-profile matches against other clubs with illustrious histories such as Newcastle and Sunderland. I sensed we might face a disadvantage in fulfilling no fewer than eight Yorkshire derby matches against Sheffield United, Bradford City, Hull City and Barnsley. Then, there were the journeys into the relatively unknown to venues like Bournemouth, Plymouth and Port Vale. Leeds were the big-hitters being set up on a pedestal ready for the coconut shy to commence.

We also had a potential problem at Elland Road with the ground-sharing policy with Hunslet Rugby League team. Based on what had happened the previous season, I feared the pitch surface might have deteriorated by the crucial spring run-in. We could not take the risk of relying solely on a pass and move game that had served Notts County so well when we had won promotion.

It was with all these things in mind that I decided to buy Vinnie Jones from Wimbledon in a £650,000 deal. I knew we needed organisation and planning to achieve our goal. I knew our approach had to be hard and firm. Any suggestion of a weakness or a brittle disposition would have been exploited by our rivals. I needed players with proven, durable character who could cope with the demands ahead. They would have to put aside personal satisfaction to get on with the task of winning at those unfashionable football outposts. They had to be players with the 'big club' temperament, capable of dealing with the potentially massive peaks and troughs of the coming campaign.

Vinnie, the former hod carrier, had appeared in the Wimbledon team and won an FA Cup Winner's medal with them. He appeared to be a Jekyll and Hyde character. In the media he seemed to relish inflating his madcap, Desperate Dan image and yet those intimate to his real nature claimed that was all sham. Dave Bassett, his old manager at Plough Lane, spoke glowingly of the boy. We began to keep tabs on a player who was rapidly becoming a legend for all the wrong reasons. There were those who said he couldn't pass water and shouldn't be allowed to roam a football field, that with every attempted pass he committed grievous bodily harm to the football.

I began to sense that inside the shaven, glowering, supposed hard-man's head there was the hint of a footballer trying to get out. I must confess, witnessing at first hand the hoped for transformation of Vinnie from an ugly duckling into a swan was not my main reason for signing him. I had concluded that Vinnie was a man with the abundant self-confidence, assertiveness and downright ego to operate in the pressure cooker atmosphere that would be part of Leeds' forthcoming season. I could also see Jones as a vital back-up to Gordon Strachan. Strachan was unquestionably our skipper and he possessed a big club temperament but I wasn't sure if he could emerge on top physically in most Second Division games to provide that vital creative spark we would undoubtedly need. Vinnie could help Gordon to galvanise the team without ever undermining the old man's status as our captain and senior professional.

People talk of give and take in negotiations. When you do business with Wimbledon, you do the giving and Sam Hamman does the taking. The Jones fee did seem high but I convinced my managing director Bill Fotherby that it was a good deal for us because it would prove to be the price of promotion. In many respects Vinnie was a pleasant surprise. In terms of a genuine servant of the football club you couldn't wish to meet a better professional. He was never late, his attitude to training was exemplary and his willingness to visit hospitals and work with the disadvantaged was first-rate.

There was one particular training session during the early build-up to pre-season that proved difficult for many of the lads. They were involved in a three and a half mile run and for much of it Vinnie was out at the front. Predictably, Strachan overtook him in the closing stages and Vinnie fell away to finish fourth. He was bitterly disappointed, yet as soon as he had recovered he was up and bringing home the back markers with words of encouragement. In general, he was nothing like the Vinnie Jones media monster he had helped to create.

Unfortunately, away from football and in his mad moments, he could be a problem. He did seem too willing to live up to his larger than life image. On two or three occasions I had to sort out off-the-field problems and make it clear to Vinnie, in no uncertain terms, precisely where he stood. There was also a problem once in a game which I had to deal with at half-time. I made my feelings clear and pointed out what I expected from Leeds players. Behaviour of that sort is not right, nor is it efficient. In the short term and long term it costs points.

As I tried to explain on more than one occasion, there is always some young buck who fancies his chances and sooner or later one of them is proved right. For a notorious bad boy to be cautioned just twice in a season with Leeds is not a bad record and, overall, he proved to be the man for the job. He enjoyed a terrific sense of camaraderie with those around him. He even overcame some withering verbal put-downs from the skipper who relished the opportunity to silence Vinnie when he was proffering some of his more off-beat views on how matches should be won. I have to say, every time he was put down mercilessly, and some times it happened far more violently in verbal and emotional terms than any kick or blow, Vinnie bounced back and didn't bear a grudge.

When Vinnie joined Leeds I thought he wanted to be both a star footballer and a public personality. I had him in my office early on and told him I was disappointed with his performances because he seemed to talk a better game off the field than he played on it.

This was during the period when he popped up as a guest on the Terry Wogan show and I told him quite candidly that he would have to decide whether he wanted to be a television personality or a footballer. I still believe he can make a living from either but I'm convinced he can't do both. I goaded him that I didn't care which he chose – which was a diplomatic white lie – but that the decision was in his hands. The next day he came back to see me to tell me he was going to concentrate his energies on football. And being the person he is, he did just that.

There's been much talk of Vinnie being a hard man. In the purely physical sense I never saw him as that. Besides being a coach and manager I've had experience of life outside football and on one of the occasions I worked on a building site I came across the hardest man I've ever encountered, who was a plasterer's labourer. Each morning we would meet the contractor's van at seven o'clock to go to the site. If you weren't there on time you were left behind because no-one was indispensable . . . except Jack that is. If Jack was absent at muster time we would take the van around to his house and knock him up. While Jack got ready the van and occupants would wait patiently outside because Jack was the finest plasterer's labourer you've ever seen.

I used to struggle to keep one plasterer going. Jack would carry hod after hod and work for three craftsmen. The physical discomfort he could put up with and the mental torture in terms of boredom he endured surpassed anything Vinnie, or any other footballer, is asked to cope with. Jack was hard.

Bryan Robson, the captain of Manchester United and England, was, in my opinion, one of the hardest players around during the Eighties. The number of contact injuries he sustained proved that. He was fearless, never seeing or appreciating the danger until he suffered.

In football terms Strachan is hard too, and not because he kicks and hurts or breaks the laws. Standing five feet six inches he knows he will get beaten in the air, that he can't really tackle and that if a game becomes overtly physical he will have to battle or go under. Yet Gordon is hard in the sense that he mentally faces this prospect before every game and backs himself to achieve success. He can cope with everything the hammer throwers might aim at him and still float to the surface to impose his level of skill on the proceedings.

In my opinion, the real physical hard men are the genuine good tacklers and single-minded headers – for instance, former Derby County and England centre-back Roy McFarland. He may never have been branded a hard man but to my mind he epitomised what the hard-man tag really stands for. He had pace and was a great header and when he hit people with his exquisitely timed tackles they knew they had encountered a real footballing force. I would argue that hard in football means the ability to compete within the laws while utilising physical power effectively. In that sense I didn't mark Vinnie down as a hard man because he didn't have a good tackling technique and had to concentrate when challenging for headers.

There are some players who, when they jump in aerial combat, only see that ball – nothing gets in their way. Our centre-back Chris Fairclough epitomises that approach.

Consequently, anything that's in his way gets moved, some-times quite violently, as he leaps to head the ball. That's hard. Vinnie was really a street fighter. He was frightened of nobody and no situation. On a football field, though, that's not enough.

When he left Leeds to team up again with Dave Bassett at Sheffield United he had done everything that had been asked of him. He became a better player than many people gave him credit for. He could follow orders, play for a team, and his contribution to Leeds' Second Division Champion-ship success should not be undervalued. But Vinnie could never live in the shadows and with the change of emphasis following our promotion I could see a long-term situation where he would not get into the first team. Vinnie would not have been able to handle that for long.

I put the Sheffield United deal to him and, at that time, he was not very pleased. I was certain though that the transfer was best for the player and the club and insisted it went through. However, even in his days of bitter disappointment there were still moments of rich fun with Vinnie. We started our first season back in Division One with an away game at Everton and I told the players before the coach left for Merseyside on the Friday afternoon my intended line-up. Everyone knew Vinnie was dropped. The rest of the travel-ling party was on board waiting to depart when word spread that Vinnie was missing. There were even suggestions that he might have done a runner.

Suddenly, Vinnie bounded onto the coach brandishing his very expensive, custom-built, double barrel shot-gun and shouted, 'I don't want you to take this too personally, gaffer, but if I'm not back in the team for Tuesday's match against Manchester United you might find yourself sleeping with the fishes.'

Possessing the resilience to immediately recover from the kind of set-backs that can undermine the confidence of any team is a vital ingredient of a successful club. I've mapped out elsewhere the way we responded to a 4-0 drubbing at Manchester City and, with just five games of the campaign remaining, went on to lift the First Division title. After all the pre-season hype and predictions we launched our bid to escape Division Two with a 5-2 defeat at Newcastle – the worst opening day result of my life.

Jack Gibson, the revered Australian Rugby League coach, once offered the sound advice that, 'A closed mouth gathers no foot.' Unfortunately, in the sporting press it can become too easy to slide into wild predictions of success tomorrow before today's challenges have even been faced, never mind overcome. The anticipation-level around Elland Road had not been pumped up by the manager or players. The predictions of glory were outside our control. I prefer the philosophy that if you don't predict too much you don't have to take too much back.

Newcastle gave us an almighty thumping and Vinnie, watching the game from the bench, was severely beaten on points in his personal little war of words with United manager Jim Smith. It may be stated, with the benefit of hindsight and knowledge of a happy ending, that the defeat at St James's Park proved to be one of the best things that could have happened to us. The incumbents of the bus travelling south from Newcastle were not a happy band of pilgrims. We had taken a hiding and the hype balloon had been well and truly pricked. We were on our backsides and facing up to life in the real world.

We then put together a 15-match unbeaten League run that lifted us to the top, just behind Sheffield United. By mid-December we had overtaken Bassett's boys at the summit and were due to meet them at Bramall Lane on Boxing Day. We earned a creditable 2-2 draw and much of the planning that went into that game became even more important for the return fixture on Easter Monday because, in between times, we slipped into some bad habits, inhibited, it seemed, by a fear of failure.

Instead of trying to win matches we went out with the sole intention of trying to avoid defeat. We were guilty of dismissing possession. Mistakenly, we thought that just knocking the ball in the general direction of their goal and effort alone were enough to get results. We stopped playing and while our results were hardly cataclysmic we were being hauled back towards the pursuing pack. A 3-1 defeat by an inspired Oldham side at Boundary Park on Good Friday was not the start to the vital Easter programme we had been hoping for.

Winning promotion from the old-style Division Two is one of the toughest tasks in English football. I never thought Leeds would capitulate completely but we were certainly making life hard for ourselves by the time our rivals from Sheffield arrived at Elland Road for the Bank Holiday fixture, desperate to exploit our recent frailties. This was a definite six-pointer for us. At Bramall Lane in the first meeting we had unsettled their goalkeeper Simon Tracey by placing a man in front of him to prevent his long drop-kicks downfield – a vital part of United's attacking strategy at that time. The goalie had been United's prime play-maker in some away games with his huge punts into the opposition penalty area. Tracey's volatile temperament began to show through, revealing a weakness that might, perhaps, prove crucial in the return.

One of his kicks was charged down and he pulled back Bobby Davison to concede a penalty *en route* to our 4-0 victory. From that day on, even though we could never totally relax, we had conquered our nerves. There would be no embarrassing surrender now.

In the immediate aftermath of Bournemouth I was particularly delighted for our Chairman Leslie Silver: he had displayed a commendably cool head throughout and whenever there were disappointments along the way he would take time to pat me on the back and quietly reassure me of his continuing faith in our battle plan. In fact, preferring a low profile in moments of triumph but finding time for those supportive words of reassurance on the bad days is both an insight and tribute to Leslie's approach to his job. I will always recall his advice in the dark days following Bournemouth when the club seemed to be under attack from all sides. He told me he had found in life that for every bad thing that happens to you there are a thousand good things, so long as you looked for them and, above all, kept your spirits intact. So, we retained our dignity and, as the Chairman predicted, justice was eventually done when we received the honours we had so deservedly earned.

There were exhausted heroes sprawled all around the visitors' dressing-room at Dean Court. Veteran keeper Mervyn Day had feared he would be rapidly replaced when I took over 19 months earlier yet produced some thrilling saves in that season and, with his accurate distribution, set up so many incisive attacks and goals. I doubt if there is any goalie in the League in recent years who could match Mervyn's radar-operated kicking. Right-back Mel Sterland, one of the band who had served me at Hillsborough as well as Elland Road, was his usual, lovable self. Is there a better attacking full-back around? Chris Kamara, that super-fit midfield tyro, shed some tears. Peter Haddock, in my opinion our most consistent player during the campaign, dropped his monosyllabic approach to offer what was, relative to him, a speech. 'Well done, gaffer,' he pronounced.

Lee Chapman, signed from Nottingham Forest to score the vital goals when we were losing direction in January, had duly completed his 21-match season for us with an impressive 12 goals – including the one that sealed victory at Bournemouth. Leeds had won the title but knowing Chappy I realised he would get just as much delight from having scored the goal that took us up. That is not a criticism. It just reflects the all-consuming nature of the prolific goal-scoring beast.

The players were sent to Magaluf on holiday as a thank-you for their efforts and winger John Hendrie, now playing for Middlesbrough, was the butt of a series of jokes after injury had forced him to miss the climax to the campaign. For a few weeks prior to this John had been teased that there was nothing really wrong with him and as a rejoinder to his team-mates he used to push an imaginary wheel-barrow around the treatment room. When asked what he was doing the Scotsman replied, 'I'm pushing my barrowload of money.'

With a few drinks in their bellies it's amazing to see the miraculous recoveries staged by some people. On the beach at Magaluf, Hendrie performed the wonderful feat of regaining full fitness to win the sprints in the Olympics being staged by the players.

And finally, the wager I had invested – at fairly sizeable odds – on Leeds to win the Second Division title had come up trumps. The only thing I didn't need was one question in the Press conference after our Bournemouth victory. 'How will Leeds cope in the First Division next season, Howard?' Even in our moment of glory we were having to face new challenges.

Chapter 7

LIVING WITH THE REVIE LEGEND

'The old photos had become emotional crutches.'

The most controversial decision I have made as manager of Leeds was to order the removal of the glory years photographs that adorned the walls of the Elland Road foyer. I meant no disrespect to the late Don Revie or the players he brought to the club and worked with in such brilliant and single-minded fashion. But those pictorial memories of yesteryear appeared to me to be an emotional crutch which too many people associated with the club had been prepared to rely on in times of adversity.

The Revie era is not only a massive part of Leeds' tradition, it laid the foundations for the future with the modern stadium Don had the foresight to help plan and develop. But I sensed there was a tendency, after years in the doldrums, for some people to recall those happy days and stare at the old photos rather than create new goals and look to the future. The memorabilia was a consolation. It should have been an inspiration.

This business of living in the past is not only associated with Leeds. The likes of Manchester United, Liverpool and Everton have had to cope with it and when compared with, say, Arsenal's proud history Leeds are veritable newcomers to success. Tradition is worthless though if you focus on the past. You must have a vision for the future and the desire to enrich your club's reputation even more.

The stripping of the walls was a symbolic act that I knew would not go unnoticed. I realised some observers would not understand my reasons while others branded it a sacrilege but I judged it very important that I provoke a reaction and shake some people out of their cosy existences inside the club. The status and tradition of being employed by Leeds was a double-edged sword. It can prove attractive when trying to sell the club to potential new signings but, when I took over, I sensed life was too easy for some. The wage structure was as good as any club in the Second Division and better than many in the top flight. The car park was full of sponsored cars and yet the team was heading towards the Third Division.

I needed to make an immediate impression inside the club and stamp a new hallmark on the place and the players. Not only were the old pictures removed, the new team was challenged to provide its own memorable moments to replace them. There would and could be no more living in, and off, the past. I told the players, 'The graveyards are full of history – and nothing moves there, either.'

I also had to deal with the backroom staff I had inherited. Manager Billy Bremner had gone to make way for me. He had been sacked. I took my time about other personnel decisions but I felt coach Norman Hunter's association with the Revie era, and players and managers since then, would create difficulties for me, in the short term, in making the immediate changes I believed were necessary. It was no disrespect to Norman's ability as a coach but, like so many before him, he became a victim of circumstances at the time.

I viewed the ground the day after my appointment with Chairman Leslie Silver, managing director Bill Fotherby and coach Peter Gunby, who had been caretaker-manager. The overall situation was worse than I had imagined. The training ground, adjacent to the stadium, was a mess. It appeared to be used by all and sundry – Leeds United, Hunslet Rugby

Howard Wilkinson in pre-season training

The Skipper – and the most influential player I've ever worked with:
Gordon Strachan (© Varley Picture Agency, Leeds)

Vinnie Jones – inside the shaven head a footballer was trying to get out

Garry Speed and David Batty – home-produced players who did so much to make Leeds champions – celebrate another great goal (© Varley Picture Agency, Leeds)

Eric Cantona – the French import who won over the fans and became a cult figure
(© Varley Picture Agency, Leeds)

A winning team . . . and the chairman hangs on to the cheque.
From left – Leslie Silver (chairman), Howard Wilkinson, Bill Fotherby (managing-
director), Peter Gilman (vice-chairman), Gordon Strachan (captain)
(© Varley Picture Agency, Leeds)

I was speechless . . . but I could still enjoy a glass of champagne.
Howard Wilkinson celebrating Leeds United's Championship triumph
(© Steve Ellis, Sheffield)

The Wilkinson boys celebrate. Howard and his sons Damian and Ben (front)
(© Steve Ellis, Sheffield)

Now that's what I call long ball football
(© David Muscroft Photography, Sheffield)

Marseille coach Raymond Goethals and Howard Wilkinson talk tactics at the Italian
FA's Coach of the Year summit (© Express Newspapers)

League, the young players and anyone else who turned up. There was neither security nor privacy with large sections of fencing being in a state of collapse. It was not a place conducive to the high standards I believe you need to see around you at your place of work every day. It is better now, but not good enough by a long way. Don't get me wrong. I'm not saying that good facilities and good equipment guarantee a good team. But I'm convinced that if you want high standards of performance from people, you have to surround them with high standards. Excellence has to become the norm in their lives, not the exception.

Marching inside the stadium I discovered things weren't any better. The dressing-rooms had not been improved for many years. The only changes were due to wear and tear and general deterioration. The changing facilities, toilet facilities, laundry where the kit was cleaned were all in a state of disrepair. The club had been run by people who were ex-Leeds players and over a number of years they had become accustomed, perhaps blind is a more fitting word, to what was happening around them. It was like owning an old car. Familiarity breeds contempt. If it was good enough for the old Leeds boys it was good enough for the new wave.

Taken in its entirety the stadium had an aura similar to an old museum. It deserved your respect for the famous old objects it housed and memories it represented but all that was tangible was history. As the years went by the memories of Revie's great team grew fonder. Aspirations for the future appeared to dim.

Predictably, some of the Revie old boys took the shilling and whenever they have wanted an easy pay day they had the opportunity to make comparisons between the new Leeds team and its title triumph and the one that achieved that feat twice for Don. Comparisons like that are, I suppose, an entertaining exercise for some but prove nothing. Life today is never as fine as the 'good old days'. It never was, nor ever will be.

Ironically, last season Leeds may, for once, have been the beneficiaries of the kind of crowded fixture programme that used to haunt Revie's team. Certainly, we were victims so often in the past. But when you consider the congestion Manchester United, our main rivals for the title, and other teams like Southampton and Nottingham Forest faced at crucial stages of the season, it really did highlight the need for re-structuring football's top division.

It was ridiculous that Manchester United should have to play four crucial games in the space of six days, just as towards the end of the season Southampton fulfilled three fixtures in five days. Brian Clough's team battled through to face Southampton in the unsung Zenith Data Cup final at Wembley and also reached the more prestigious Rumbelows League Cup final against Manchester United. By the time they reached the big showdown Forest were physically shot and had players carrying injuries. They were also without their inspirational skipper Stuart Pearce, sidelined with a knee injury. That fixture pile-up before the League Cup final prevented Forest from giving of their best in a football show-piece – and that is not good for the game.

The pursuit of honours should not be just about winning and losing: we should also be encouraged in our pursuit of excellence and the ability to show how good a team is when put to a sensible test. Everyone at Leeds will sympathise with my views because I'm sure no other club over the years has paid the price in terms of bitter disappointment and set-backs that we did due to maladministration and fixture chaos. In fact, it was back in 1970 that Revie's team faced eight games in the space of just 14 days as they pursued glory on three fronts. Inevitably, even Don's great side found that kind of programme too daunting and fell between all three stools.

Last season Manchester United's League campaign faltered as they faced five games in ten days. They won the first, drew the second and then lost three on the trot. It was demeaning that the destiny of such a special prize could be decided in such a way. Yet Revie's boys had lived through that nightmare on more than one occasion.

Billy Bremner was skipper of the Leeds team that must be ranked as one of the truly great English club sides of the post-war period and that went on to win trophies and earn esteem across Europe. The years Leeds spent at the top during Don's reign demanded that they must be afforded the greatest respect. In fact, since the Second World War I believe only two clubs have laid the right foundations and enjoyed the potential to be really successful on a long-term basis – Leeds and Liverpool. Liverpool have stayed at the top for 30 years while Leeds slipped by the wayside in the mid-Seventies.

Leeds missed out for two reasons. We were found lacking in the boardroom and Don Revie left to become England manager. This club started to die the minute Don was allowed to depart. If he had stayed I honestly believe Leeds could have enjoyed the kind of supremacy that has made Liverpool an institution in European football.

I don't think the Anfield directors would have allowed their top manager to depart in the way Don left Leeds. Approaches from the Football Association for Revie were entirely predictable. The Leeds hierarchy should have ensured he had nothing to gain by considering a job away from Elland Road. Unfortunately, Don's relatively unsuccessful spell as England manager, and the manner of his departure, have somewhat diminished his achievements and the impression he made in the development of the game in this country. He was a highly successful, imaginative, innovative thinker and it's a tragedy that the change of direction he took in management and his early death deprived many of us of the benefit of his experience.

I welcomed wholeheartedly the club's plans to open an official museum at Elland Road. I immediately suggested that all the old photographs should be given pride of place there along with tributes to the Revie days. But it will be just as important that the winning of the Second Division title in 1990 and the crowning of Leeds as 1992 League champions merits its own little corner. A whole generation of Leeds fans had never known what it was like to support a successful side. They know now and let's hope this is just the start of a bright future that extends beyond my career in management.

There is a great desire to maintain progress at Leeds, both on and off the pitch. Just as our pursuit of the League title reached its climax the directors were formally approving the construction of the biggest cantilever stand in the world on the Lowfields Road side of the ground. While the move towards all-seater stadia has inevitably reduced the capacity of most grounds our crowd limit will be increased once the giant new stand is fully operational next season.

The total redevelopment of Elland Road was part of Don's dream for the club. He left and the genuine hope of fulfilling that dream probably went with him. We are edging back towards creating the super stadium the club deserves and we will deservedly provide a venue when England hosts the European Championships in 1996.

Elland Road has been described on many occasions as the most intimidating ground in English football. Certainly, the noise level is high but I don't believe the crowd makes a team. In fact, the opposite is true, the team makes a crowd. And, I must also point out, many visiting players are inspired by the atmosphere inside our ground. There may be some who don't relish the experience but the great players don't just cope, they thrive on it.

Before the season that marked our return to the First Division we had a meeting to discuss ways of staging matches in the most dramatic fashion and it was agreed that we should search for an anthem to mark the Leeds team's entrance before the match and after half-time. The con-sensus eventually backed Bill Fotherby's suggestion to use the theme music from the film *Rocky*. That idea provoked much debate, with the club accused of whipping up the fans' fervour.

We held a Press call at Elland Road in the summer before the following campaign and asked the assembled journalists for suggestions on how we could further improve the image of the club. Bob Cass, of the *Mail on Sunday*, explained his objections to the *Rocky* theme and called for change. Eventually, we opted for a combination of *Fanfare for the Common Man* and the theme music from *Chariots of Fire*. That seemed to appease everybody but there was still to emerge a certain irony about our game of musical chairs. When we used *Rocky* and Elland Road was supposed to be at its most intimidating we lost five home games in the season. The following year, with the softly-softly approach, we were the only club in the Football League to enjoy an invincible home record. I'm grateful to Bob Cass for his assistance.

Chapter 8

FOOTBALL'S BERMUDA TRIANGLE

'It appears the real blueprint has disappeared without trace in football's very own Bermuda Triangle.'

Just six weeks after celebrating Leeds United's League Championship glory I was on the brink of resigning my job and walking away from English football.

Thankfully, my discontent had nothing to do with my employers at Elland Road but, after returning from the Italian FA's coaching seminar at Corverciano to the scenario of dissatisfaction and disorganisation engulfing English football, I experienced a sense of utter frustration bordering on dismay.

I had spoken with some of Europe's top coaches like Fabio Capello of AC Milan, Raymond Goethals from Marseille and Bobby Robson, then about to leave the Dutch champions PSV Eindhoven to work in Portugal. Their collective experiences made me realise there is a much better way of running football abroad, where players are basically asked to produce their peak form once a week and where the coach or manager can concentrate on getting matters right on the field. The kind of sane approach towards a blue riband league within their domestic football was already in operation. To us in England it remained a distant pipedream.

The contrast with life in England could not have been more marked. The canvas we were being ordered to paint on was so blemished. The promises of a bright future were again evaporating as so many chairmen snatched the chance of a fast buck and ignored the greater good of improving the state of English football. I came home to the rows over the constitution of the Premier League, the botched television deal with BSkyB and a growing awareness that, despite all the public plaudits we had received, the League Managers' Association's sensible, cogent, pragmatic views on football's future were once again going to be ignored. My chagrin degenerated to the point of dejection. As Chairman of the new association I had become disgruntled at the way so many managers, myself included, had given up hours of our private time and energy to travel around the country meeting representatives of the Football League, the Premier League, the Press and referees' societies. We had been invited to talk and were continually told, particularly by the establishment figures, that consultations were necessary. Unfortunately, we were only to find that by May 1992 all the areas we had discussed, and to which we felt we could offer a worthwhile input, had been ignored.

Basically, I felt so many managers had been wasting their time and that we were standing in the path of a massive bureaucratic snowball that was inexorably heading our way. The impulsion from the get-rich-quick brigade was so great there was little we could do to stop it. I also felt sympathy for England manager Graham Taylor as he prepared to take the England team to the European Championships in Sweden. He was well aware, no matter what happened in the finals, that he would face two more haphazard years attempting to cope with the hurdles placed in front of him by the Premier League to guide England to the 1994 World Cup finals in the United States.

Graham would have been aware that during the period of frantic qualification his best players would be expected to play more competitive football in England than ever before in a more cramped fixture list. Yet, before its inception, the perpetrators of the Premier League ethos were so keen to promote it on the grounds of revolutionising our football future out of all recognition. Clearly, along the way, the plans for the brave new world had been shredded.

If an independent employment agency was asked to recruit the men in football with the widest knowledge of the sport and the ability to guide the industry into the 21st century there is no question their selection would include a high proportion of football managers. The different factions may squabble about football's future but it is the members of the League Managers' Association who have proposed the soundest ideas to improve the game and the clearest vision for the future. We have shown, particularly during the debate surrounding the television deal last summer and the advent of the Premier League, that we can see beyond the vested interests of our clubs towards a future which is better for everyone. Sadly, that same maxim cannot be applied to many other people in football.

At the very time that football was splitting into new groupings with the Premier League breakaway from the Football League, the Managers' Association was established to represent the men at the cutting edge of the game in both Leagues. In fact, the vast majority of our Premier League members – such as George Graham, Brian Clough, Ron Atkinson and I – have served smaller clubs during our managerial grounding. We have worked on shoestring budgets and faced the grim realities of living week-to-week because of budget difficulties and the like.

Managers are in the main former professional players. They understand the psyche of the players. They have the priceless gift of experience. In many cases, time, intelligence and pure, native wit have combined to distil that experience into great wisdom. Obviously, any move inside to an executive position brings about the need to become versed in the rule book and more detailed financial matters. But, given the comprehensive duties performed by most managers in this country, such knowledge is acquired anyway during the course of five or ten years' employment. Most directors have no background in football. Most players have no knowledge of finance and organisation at this level. Most administrators have no comprehension of the potentially nerve-shattering atmosphere in which you live and work when your job security is decided by a team's results. You have to display foresight, initiative, insight, decisiveness, the ability to organise and, above all, courage . . . or you are doomed.

It is the managers who can give such a constructive and priceless input to the game. I thought it was a major long-term benefit when we set up the new organisation in 1991 and I was honoured to be the inaugural Chairman, yet we found the many calls for more manager involvement in the decision-making process in the game to be, on too many occasions, merely a lip service exercise. We were involved in consultative discussions on all manner of issues during the 12 months leading up to the launch of the Premier League. I now have to concede, hand on heart, looking at the decisions that have been taken, it would appear most of what we said was totally ignored.

We analysed the Football Association's discussion document *Blueprint for the Future* and these talks emphasised the way our membership looked beyond their own backyard. Despite the fact that some of our members would lose their status as top flight managers under the proposals, the vast majority voted in favour of reducing the First Division/ Premier League to 18 clubs. We saw the reduced fixture list as a definite advantage in trying to produce better quality football with players allowed longer to prepare and practice between matches. Yet it appears the real blueprint has disappeared without trace, a victim of what can only be described as football's very own Bermuda Triangle. It's not the first such disappearance. Sadly, it won't be the last either. The decision-makers didn't get where they are today through not knowing how to drown even the very best future plans and schemes in a sea of selfishness, self-interest, confusion and downright stupidity. Reginald Perrin, eat your heart out.

When the Premier League announced the £304 million television deal with BSkyB and BBC in May 1992 many in football rubbed their hands gleefully at the prospect of pennies from heaven. From around £14 million per annum under the old contract with ITV we were suddenly going to benefit by as much as a five-fold increase. It sounded too good to be true . . . and it was. The idea that there would be 30 live Sunday and 30 live Monday fixtures was totally non-sensical and impossible to fulfil. Given the already stipulated agreement of four blank weekends for international preparations, FA Cup dates and European club involvement, and the genuine possibility in this country of a weather-enforced shut-down, the only thing the Premier League could really promise the television moguls was a state of total chaos. It makes you wonder why nobody at any time said, 'Hang on a minute, let's examine the practicalities of these proposals. Can they really work? Moreover, is what we're contemplating really in the best interests of football in this country?' The chaos spluttered into the public domain when the fixture list was published. Could the League and the television company really be serious in thinking Manchester City could play Queen's Park Rangers live on a Monday night and then expect Gerry Francis's team to rush home in the early hours of Tuesday morning to prepare for a game against Southampton at Loftus Road on the Wednesday night?

When Manchester United manager Alex Ferguson and I spoke out so vehemently against the deal, the television companies, who genuinely thought they had tabled a good offer and wanted to enjoy healthy co-operation with the clubs, were obviously hurt. Furthermore, I would have thought they would be even more annoyed when they understood our reasons and the fact that such obvious political problems had not been pointed out to them during negotiations. Leeds and Manchester United's antipathy to the contract was supported by Liverpool, Arsenal, Everton and Aston Villa. We all sent official letters to the Premier League Chairman Sir John Quinton explaining why our clubs would refuse to play in the Monday night matches. It was soon after this that I hosted a meeting at Elland Road with the sports hierarchy from BSkyB that provided a revealing insight into the lack of leadership within football.

Dave Hill, Sky's head of sport, and Vic Wakeling, their football editor, were keen to establish why I was so vehemently opposed to their deal. I pointed out two facts: that all League managers believed there was too much televised football; and that from a totally practical point of view Monday night fixtures were a horrendous mistake. Obviously, the view that there was too much televised football was purely our opinion and we accepted it as such. The Sky team might beg to differ.

I explained my fears that when we wanted to put a good, exciting product on television our chances of fulfilling that objective were paradoxically being undermined by the very demands of the television deal. Ideally, teams should play just once a week, giving players the opportunity to recover from the exertions of their previous outing. The bigger clubs were now concerned that they would have to play on Monday and Wednesday nights to complete their League and cup programmes with the potential for a rift between the old Football League, governors of the League Cup, and the Football Association/Premier League powerbase, a handicap that we could all foresee emerging. In essence, the marriage of the Premier League and the massive new television contract, with all its promises of a bright new age, was self-defeating. There were raised eyebrows all round as Dave Hill recognised the implications of the deal his overlords had done.

I'm sure Dave Hill was astounded that the Chairmen and people in power had not investigated their proposals and the ramifications of the transaction. I'm also sure Dave suddenly realised he had an awful lot to learn. Football has had this tremendous capacity to shoot itself in the foot for years and is getting better at it the more practice it gets. 'Take the money and run' is almost football's motto.

The annoying aspect to all this was that back in August 1991 I, on behalf of the League Managers' Association, had been raising these same points to, among others, Rick Parry, the Premier League's inaugural chief executive, at our consultative meetings. There was much to commend in many of Rick's views, not least the way in which the NFL had dramatically changed its flagging image and prospects in the United States. If the Premier League could adopt a similar approach, what exciting times would surely be on the horizon. Rick's admiration and deep knowledge of the American ways of doing things was well justified. Crucial to grid iron's renaissance some 20 years earlier had been the change of approach by the television companies. The introduction of the 'Monday Match' had revolutionised viewing habits and stimulated the growth of a whole new section of American football supporters. In theory, the adoption of the masterplan appeared sound. Unfortunately, a couple of little details were to make a whole world of difference.

Leeds United won the League title by playing 42 League games. There was disappointment in many quarters because we were only involved in seven cup-ties. In our previous season we played in 60 games. If you study the NFL fixture list you discover that the teams play a minimum of eight home and eight away games. The finalists in the Super Bowl accumulate just 19 appearances in reaching the summit of their sport in a season that runs from September to the end of January.

The NFL would never contemplate a deal with a cable or satellite television company that could not guarantee beaming the pictures into every home in the United States. Secondly, if a team is selected to play three times on the Monday night they can then ask for a switch back to Sunday because the coaches and players see the fact that they are losing one day's preparation for the next match as crucial to their season. They demand a six-day build-up to games rather than five. Imagine how they would cope with the regular demand facing English managers and their clubs of completing three vital games in the space of seven days.

I also discussed finance with Hill. The PFA, the players' union, had reached an agreement with the Football League in the past and the new Premier League to receive a cut from the television contract. In an effort to see the LMA in working operation as an effective organisation I asked for the same. We hadn't got their power. But power was not, and is not, what we're after. We have enough problems dealing with the individual powers inside our clubs. But we think we should have the potential to influence, for all the reasons I've listed, the future of football. We sought a fair share of the television monies but Dave Hill replied that after ploughing so much into the contract he couldn't see his bosses being prepared to put money into the LMA.

I reiterated that the money should come from them. We didn't want the cash to be forwarded via the Premier League to us because we didn't want Premier League club chairmen dictating as to where the money should go and how it should be spent. Neither did we want to operate under threat of sudden censure. We wanted to be independent and give unbiased opinions that always remained outside and above vested interests.

Ironically, our negotiations with ITV had gone much smoother and, had they won the contract, part of the deal would have confirmed a guaranteed percentage to the LMA. I suggested to Rick Parry that he should think along the same lines. He should make it clear the managers would be involved with the funds emanating from television and not internal Premier League coffers. Unfortunately, once again the situation had been allowed to slide along and, at this moment, probably rests in some nice, quiet cul de sac. Our position had been taken for granted. We had been disregarded as a body and seen as a group who, because of the insecurity of our individual positions, would meekly fall into line as soon as games started to be played. We believe that sort of thinking has been prevalent far too long. Surely it cannot continue if, as all concerned are fond of stating repeatedly, 'It's the game's interests we have at heart.'

We had 93 members working in the field at the start of the 1991-92 campaign. One-third of them were sacked or replaced during that season. Yet, here we were with the big guns like George Graham at Arsenal, Liverpool's Graeme Souness and Alex Ferguson operating on behalf of their colleagues in the Football League. In no sense could we be accused of being élitist.

The LMA has to win the payment battle otherwise how could we help our members in all sorts of ways, in particular those unsung managers who are ditched by their clubs and left waiting for months for contracts to be honoured? Football management can be very well paid but it has its casualties. Many more than most people imagine. We feel we have a responsibility to them and to the game which is our passionate hobby, our love and our life. Divide and rule has been the watchword in football for too long.

The BSkyB team were not aware that some managers have the right contractually to decide who comes into the football club, who takes photographs and where, who can conduct interviews and who can be interviewed. I also revealed that my contract gave me powers that virtually allowed me to decide the positioning of television cameras – if I chose to. We didn't want a policy of no co-operation but if it was necessary . . . so be it. Some will be surprised by this knowledge but, if you think about it, it is commonsense. The manager accepts responsibility when things go wrong. He may even get the sack. Therefore, it's only right that he has the responsibility to make decisions which he feels will help things go right. The problem of payment wasn't down to me as Chairman of the LMA. They had all blithely sailed on ignoring the fact that here was another important matter that needed to be dealt with.

Dave and Vic left my office with plenty to think about. I have to confess I was no more optimistic than before. After 30 years in football you realise not a lot has changed regarding the administration of the game. The discussions had been fruitful in one sense. Dave Hill, Vic Wakeling and myself had established that most of our views on football, television and the future of the sport were very similar. As the men on the shop floor most of our working lives we had a great deal of sympathy for each other's predicament. I suppose generals feel much the same way about politicians. Nobody ever really wins in that game either.

But by this stage I had reviewed my personal state of angst. I had slept on my worries for the English game and realised it was no good running away from them. In fact, the kind of disorganisation surrounding football at present made the challenge of attaining success even greater. It may be an unfair challenge but it was there to be conquered.

One of the more controversial sections within the original FA blueprint was a proposition that formal qualifications should exist for managers, coaches and administrative staff working in the Premier League and that the qualifications should become a pre-requisite for employment at that level in the future. Those suggestions provoked intense debate and much was made of the similar conditions being operated in other countries. Germany, in particular, was cited as a potential role model at one stage. In fact, the Germans caved in on this particular issue to make sure Franz Beckenbauer could be national team manager as opposed to national coach – the title held with such distinction by the likes of Helmut Schoen and Jupp Derwall in the past. By exploiting a loophole Beckenbauer landed the national job but he would have found it much harder to get a legitimate coaching post within the Bundeslige.

The LMA was brought in for discussions about job qualifi-cations and the talks are still continuing. In a sense, I believe qualifications for jobs do exist already. Those qualifications are in people's minds when they're looking to appoint a manager or coach at their club. But, if you then look at the people making the appointments, there's a great disparity within football. Some clubs have directors and administrators of high calibre, with a reasonable perception of what can generate success in football. There are others, though, with little idea of what is necessary for their clubs. I fear that in these cases standards are low and continue to dip.

Unfortunately, in England there is no correlation between the status of the available job and the qualifications needed to get it. I've seen some of the country's most prestigious clubs making weird decisions. Education, in all walks of life, is essential. Job training, in any walk of life, is vital. How one acquires training or education doesn't matter. What does matter is that the education and training is effective.

The system of management in England does not provide sufficient opportunity for in-job training of management or coaching skills. We have an FA coaching qualification which takes two weeks in its final stages to acquire plus some preparatory work over several weekends. We've launched attempts to run management courses. Some have been suc-cessful, others not. Most job appointments are still made on the basis of personal recommendations from within the game and previous results. Most levels of education and training are self-acquired.

Judging by my travels all over the world I would state that the standard of management and coaching in England is reasonably high when one compares the training available with that in other countries. That reflects great credit on most of those involved. They have the drive and determina-tion to seek the answers for themselves to questions that could be more easily answered by the governing body.

FOOTBALL'S BERMUDA TRIANGLE

I don't think qualifications should be compulsory because in football, ultimately, managers will be judged by results – particularly those managers at the top clubs. But there is a field where a well-qualified coach, with a proven track record, should be allowed to continue about his work unhindered. I'm thinking here of the army of youth coaches, up and down the land, attempting to nurture the stars of the future. It's a fact that many managers on their arrival at a club call for an immediate clear out and dispose of all the coaching resources. Coaching appointments, especially at youth level, should be made on a better informed basis.

The acquisition and production of young players has little to do with the senior professionals and first-team results. Youth development should be divorced from that and respected as a long-term investment. There is a tendency to judge youth team coaches by impressive League form and the number of junior cup finals a team has reached. I would prefer to judge the youth coach on the number of players that he keeps to make the grade through the club's junior ranks, the quality of those players and whether they become a successful investment for the club.

Qualifications, in the sense of passing examinations, should not be essential. All that does is prove a person's ability to pass exams. Attendance on well-structured courses should be compulsory and can do nothing but improve the quality of our game – even if it's only in reducing by a fraction the number of sackings we get in a season. On many occasions those dismissals can be blamed on inexperience rather than lack of ability.

I would propose a scheme that would involve players during the last two or three years of their careers. They would attend well-organised management lectures of a type similar to those currently run by the Open University. We now have sufficient knowledge and expertise within football to staff a course of university standard. The lecturers would pass on a wealth of information to the managers of the future. In doing that the process would produce a self-regulating entrance procedure.

There are players who go into management with no idea of what the job entails and who are unaware of the personal demands they will have to face. I often fear that kind of person might end up resigning or being fired before he has even had the chance to establish himself. The past experience and collected wisdom of the lecturers on the courses would undoubtedly come into play in these situations. I believe, even in the early stages, that the wise old foxes with many years' experience in football may be able to pinpoint the player who would be better advised to opt for a 'proper job' on civvy street and also spot the man with the ability to prove a successful manager of the future.

Football in England is a multi-million-pound industry with the stakes getting even higher by the season. The amount of money turned over by our sport is quite phenomenal. It therefore seems ridiculous to me that some ex-players, however well-intended, should be appointed by directors, who don't have the football intellect to find a manager, and yet collectively allow our industry to be run on a trial and error basis. Making the wrong appointment can often adversely affect a club for years to come. Finding a manager still seems to be a matter for too much guesswork and a hypothetical visit to the directors' selection laboratory.

At the moment in England, an impressive playing career is probably the priority factor when appointing the rookie manager. As history has shown, this is absolutely no indicator of a man's ability. Imagine putting four men in a lounge adjacent to the boardroom waiting to be interviewed for the vacant manager's job. For the sake of the argument we'll make all four around the same age and suppose they are chasing their first managerial post. The names of the quartet are Bob Paisley, Brian Clough, Bobby Charlton and Bobby Moore. Who would have got the job? I have no hesitation in claiming that at the majority of clubs the order for nominations would have run: Charlton, Moore, Paisley, Clough.

The two Bobbys' popularity among the great England players of all-time would make them attractive to most directors who love a famous name in their manager's office. They may think Bob Paisley will have learned something as a player at Liverpool but Cloughie's premature, injury-enforced retirement would not have helped him.

If we look at the scenario in reality we are well aware that Charlton and Moore, great players that they undoubtedly were, never made the grade as managers. Paisley was arguably the wisest, most successful English club manager of all time and Clough's success at winning League championships at two clubs is a wonder of the modern age.

I don't suggest that vocational training will provide an aspiring manager with the wisdom of Paisley, but it would be a way of making life easier for prospective managers, it would help football run more efficiently and, overall, add to the stability and well-being of the game.

Sadly, if the consensus was to institute this kind of dramatic change it would only happen with great difficulty. Despite cosmetic changes to the Football Association, Premier League and Football League, the fact is that football is constantly ripped asunder by politics. The sooner we have one all-embracing authority in England the better. The sooner that authority acquires executive and administrative talent to conduct affairs properly the better.

It's ridiculous that far-reaching decisions should be made by committees that are constantly changing and that the constitution of the committees is so blatantly affected by club patronage and power groups. It's unfair that on so many key issues club chairmen vote on deep-rooted issues and simply elect to support their vested interests.

For the long-term good an executive should be formed and, if necessary, the members of the ruling group should be asked to sever their commitments with any club. They would be paid, independent officers of the football authority but with the experience of life within competitive club football. I would cite a mixture of senior officials such as the FA's chief executive Graham Kelly with the likes of Liverpool chief executive Peter Robinson, Ipswich manager John Lyall, Everton director Philip Carter, retired referee George Courtney and a senior PFA member to work as a unit. We would elect these officers for a minimum four-year incumbency and allow them to get on with improving the many aspects that are so clearly going wrong at present. They would make their decisions on merit, based on their knowledge and experience in football and with no axe to grind on behalf of a specific club.

It was just before Leeds and Manchester United embarked on their January match trilogy last season that Alex Ferguson travelled over to Elland Road as a member of the League Managers' Association committee to meet youth coaches from around the country. It's typical of the small-minded mentality of some folk in the game that eyebrows were raised that we should be working in tandem at a time when our clubs were about to do battle but I think our joint approach emphasises our determination to improve the quality of young players entering the game.

Leeds' and Manchester United's first teams have to win. We are judged by results. But lower down in the game, at schoolboy and youth level, a genuine crusade can, indeed must, be mounted to enhance the quality of player we produce in England. Having been sent by the FA to a series of World Cup and European Championship finals, I have tried to establish proven pointers as to why other countries appear to leave us behind in terms of technique and developing their young players.

Undoubtedly, there is a gap between the wealthy countries of Europe and the likes of Brazil, Mexico and the emerging African nations. In those poor nations football, along with boxing, still provides the primary escape route from the poverty-stricken ghettoes. The kids play football from dawn until dusk and beyond. Their natural skills are enhanced because football offers them perhaps their sole purpose in life.

We're not going to turn the clock back in Europe to days of hardship but there are still lessons for us in England to assimilate. We're all aware in football that youngsters today have so many options within their spare time to choose from. Football and cricket no longer enjoy absolute supremacy as our national sports for winter and summer. That very same problem should be handicapping the Dutch, the Germans, the French and the Danish as they search for successors to Cruyff, Beckenbauer, Platini and Morten Olsen. Travel around Germany and Holland and you're struck by the number of public and private tennis courts for instance. Certainly, the Netherlands and Germany have enjoyed far greater international continuity over a period of 20 years than any other international teams in Europe.

It was Yugoslav striker Darko Pancev who emphasised the way that in his homeland of Macedonia youngsters always wanted to work at ball skills and ways of mastering their craft before they went into a competitive match – even on a patch of waste land. The boy who couldn't trap the ball or wasted possession was taunted by his friends. Sheer skill was a sign of acceptability. As schoolteachers all over Britain will confirm, the competitive nature of our boys sees them pleading for a match as soon as they get out on the playing field. They'll willingly ignore the skills sessions to get on with winning the game 10-9. We don't want to lose that competitive streak but it does need harnessing within an environment that benefits the British game.

English football doesn't require a blueprint now. It desperately needs a blackprint. This should read like a modern Magna Carta for the game, etched in black on a tablet of stone so that not a word can be removed. The overlords I've already mentioned, who do have proven backgrounds within our national sport, should then be charged with appointing a football fuehrer whose task would be to follow through all the recommendations for the future.

In England, by the time a footballer is 25 he has been pasteurised, homogenised and virtually sterilised. Like our milk, most of them have had the cream removed. The product may last longer but it doesn't taste as good. The FA always likes to talk about the pyramid of excellence and boast that the English pyramid has the broadest base in the world. To be honest, a better comparison would be with an amorphous lump, the emphasis being on quantity rather than quality.

Our players are the most durable in world football. Their collective character is without question and is one of the most admired traits in world football. But, as the European Championships again confirmed, for the past two decades we have not produced the really gifted footballer in the numbers we should given the assertion that we do possess the raw material. Conversely, since the 1950s the Germans have produced a team every two years capable of reaching the final stages, if not winning, every major competition. Surely, there's a lesson there for us providing we have the intelligence to experiment and the courage to change.

The changes that must be made are fundamental. Cosmetic meddling is not enough. Football now requires major surgery – right across the board. Firstly, let's take the development of young players. I will happily concede that we have more youngsters registered and playing football than any other nation in the world. But is the nature of their involvement conducive to producing good players? If our failure at international level is to attract the frenzied criticism that it does then those that take the abuse should also have the right, in their own interests, to see the development of better players.

The medical reports emanating from the FA's School of Excellence at Lilleshall make appalling reading. It's ridiculous that from the best 30 or so Under-15 boys in England last year six have already developed serious back injuries, mainly from playing too much football. At Leeds we make it clear to our schoolboy signings that we don't want them even thinking about playing Saturday and Sunday matches. They are in danger of burning themselves out by over-competing.

The football fuehrer should ban 11-a-side matches for children under the age of 14 or 15, replacing them with a progressive series of small-sided games on pitches that are relative in size to the development of those teenagers. Over the past decade schools and teachers have changed dramatically. Physical education these days takes on a much wider, and probably more worthwhile, perspective in terms of its place in the school curriculum. PE teachers are not employed to produce gifted footballers for professional clubs. They are an integral part of the education process designed to turn out the sort of well-rounded child most of us would wish to have as our own son or daughter. I think, in terms of developing the better young footballers, we should take the teaching of specific major sports away from schools and into clubs – but different clubs to what we see at present.

Young track stars and budding field eventers head to an athletics club. Who can doubt the tremendous strides witnessed in this country as our best athletics coaches have adapted more professional approaches to tutoring the athletes of tomorrow? Likewise, if you want your son or daughter to be a golfer you find a good golf pro. If you want your children to be good tennis players you send them to a good tennis professional. And if one of them wants to learn how to ride a horse properly, you find a good equestrian teacher at a riding school or pony club.

If you want your boy to play football where do you send him? You might send him to one of the thousands of Sunday League clubs that have proliferated over the last 20 years – but that is not the answer. Don't get me wrong, I'm not trying to blame the perils and pitfalls of the English game on

Sunday football. I just think there are better ways of teaching young players.

Our professional football clubs have to change. The youth policy has to be divorced from the first team. There is absolutely no justification for those involved in youth football being made to pay a price when the first team suffers. Why should the youth coach be dismissed when the manager is fired? Clubs and administrators have to recognise that the development of talent is so vital to football's long-term well-being that the people who work in that area should be offered special, protected status. We need to develop a system for producing coaches whose specific aim in life is to nurture youngsters. The coaches need to be professional people and be awarded high esteem within the system.

The very nature of the football club will have to undergo radical changes. At present, the club essentially means the first team. In my opinion, though, the first-team players should stand and exist on their own. Youngsters, in vast numbers, should come into the club and be catered for by people who've undergone a thorough training programme specifically designed for the purpose.

In the past clubs have been accused of simply searching for the best boys and turning their backs on the rest. That approach is wrong. We must take a wider view than that. We have to attract kids and make them believe, whatever their ability, that they have a right to play football and be looked after in a proper manner. It happens in other parts of the world, in countries which have far fewer advantages than we have here.

Each football club should become a pyramid in itself. A pyramid of activity and teaching where the cream – without pressure, with a reduced level of competition – gradually rises to the top.

The concept of the professional game in England will also have to change. I'm convinced that at present we're trying to support too many jobs for too many people. Professional football is an élitist activity. It isn't a fair world. Indeed, for football to be healthy there has to be a situation of too many actors for too few jobs. The competition aspect is of fundamental importance. I honestly don't know how long we can support four divisions of full-time footballers. We may have to adapt if we are to provide the stimulus to a new system that can make football stronger and more vibrant.

At the top level I believe clubs should operate on a first-team squad system with perhaps 20 to 22 professionals who effectively form the playing staff. On this basis the reserve team would have to be scrapped. Those squad members who aren't in the first team would gain match practice through arranged friendlies. On occasions recently I've witnessed reserve matches with a team of virtual schoolboys facing opponents comprising first-team regulars, playing simply because the fixture must be fulfilled. Neither side has gained anything from that particular exercise.

The apprentice system would also be scrapped. I would introduce associate training schemes in which prospective footballers would attend training sessions at a club maybe four or five afternoons or evenings each week. As a result of these sessions, some of them would eventually be asked to join the first-team squad. That would be the big attraction for them but there would be little in the sense of an intermediate stage.

These days the massive number of young players earning amounts that, for their age, are not insubstantial can actually reduce the incentive for them to push themselves for the future. Their resolve can be weakened by the financial advantage they have over most of their contemporaries. It would be healthier if the club worked with a group of youngsters and then selected the one or two who were seen as potential senior players. Those not taken on would be free to move sideways or down the Leagues, dependent on their talent. Below the level of the cream I do see part-time football becoming widespread and regionalisation of the lower divisions a virtual certainty.

It's a tribute to the remarkable character of the British that our footballers put up with the pressures to which we subject them and manfully adapt to a way of life that would be totally alien to 90 per cent of the world's best players. The fact that we compete at all at international level reflects immense credit on the players' desire to carry out their responsibilities to their clubs, families and themselves. Unfortunately, the end product of this system is that we produce 'coping players'. They cope with all the different challenges we throw at them and become reactive in their performances. They become aces at survival.

I watched a film once called *They Shoot Horses, Don't They?* about the dance marathon craze that hit the United States in the 1920s. I have to confess that particular drama reminded me of some of the football matches that take place week in, week out in our country. Consequently, our players have no time to learn their trade or hone their skills. The coach has no time to prepare his team effectively. The League programme becomes just that – a programme, instead of a series of special events. An organised match involving two well-prepared, competing teams should be an exciting event. There should be time between games for the players, the coaches and the spectators to prepare. The game should stand out like a spectacular drama. Football shouldn't be like *Coronation Street*, a soap opera. Players shouldn't be world-weary like Ken Barlow. Our matches should be the main event. Our players should be searching to be at the pinnacle of their profession, like Frank Sinatra.

For the good of the game we also have to confront and destroy a totally unwanted football phenomenon . . . the parentatic. It's a hybrid cross – the parent who degenerates into his son's most biased fanatical follower. These are the ranting, raving people who frequently patrol the touchlines up and down the country every Saturday and Sunday, morning and afternoon, in the mistaken belief that their boy has the talent to 'go all the way'. Even if he did have the necessary ability there can be no doubt that two years of touchline tantrums will either drive him out of the game or drive the game out of him. The pursuit of tin-pot trophies and plastic medals really causes innumerable problems.

The introduction of sophisticated tactics and a win-at-all-costs mentality does little to produce the virtuoso we're all so desperately searching for. For a youngster, learning how to lose is perhaps a better maxim than learning how to win. That can come later. The children should be playing for enjoyment, for self-expression, self-satisfaction. They should be experimenting and then practising what they've discovered. Just watch a group of youngsters in a schoolyard. Whatever the game they are invariably living out fantasies. Imitation is crucial to their play. That's why it's also crucial that the idols they imitate are the very best.

This isn't the vicious circle or Catch 22 it may at first appear. As I've already stated, in England if we only possess two attributes they are potential and determination. I'm convinced, given the correct system, that we can produce the best, most intuitive, most knowledgeable teachers in the world. It would then be their duty to help develop the potential within our land.

Germany and Holland have developed some of the finest coaching schemes for youngsters. The young players are spotted at an early age and carefully nurtured. The alternative sporting attractions in both countries are immense so the football coaching has to be inventive and appealing. Physique is no excuse for a player failing to master his art either. We may think in a stereotyped environment that a six foot two inches player is going to be a stopper centre-half. In last summer's European Championships we witnessed the audacious skills of some big fellows like Marco van Basten, Ruud Gullit, Frank Rijkaard and Stefan Effenberg. You don't need to resort solely to power play utilising big men when players like that possess poise and delectable touch. I liked Gullit's phrase when he said most of his team were 'on first name terms with the ball'. Conversely, there is also room for the players of small stature. Thomas Hassler may lack inches but he was one of the most effective attacking forces in the finals.

The Taylor Report, following the Hillsborough disaster in 1989, has placed an intolerable burden on the whole of football. I'm not sure that all clubs will survive the test although there are suggestions from inside Government offices that the all-seater recommendations for lower division clubs may be relaxed. Yet, do we need all those super stadia? Could our money be better spent in different areas?

During the last three or four years the city of Sheffield has witnessed the spending of many millions of pounds on three tremendous stadia: Hillsborough and Bramall Lane – the homes of Sheffield Wednesday and Sheffield United – and the Don Valley stadium which was originally constructed for the World Student Games and features an athletics track around the pitch perimeter. Without a shadow of doubt, all three will be underused. In fact, I would guess that for 90 per cent of the week they will all be redundant.

A proposal that Wednesday and United share the same stadium would doubtless be met with cries of 'That must never happen' from Wednesday fans and 'Over my dead body' from the Blades' followers. It is a very emotional argument but in some cases people just don't have any choice. Would the fans of Aldershot or Accrington Stanley mind too much if, instead of watching no team, they had the opportunity to watch their favourites in the stadium belonging to someone else? Aldershot and Accrington would never have reached the footballing status of Wednesday and United but who knows what the future might bring for any club? I can't see there being an overall increase in the total amount of money available for investment in our stadia.

In the interests of improving the product out on our League grounds I'm now convinced we need full-time, professional referees. I would propose that senior players, in the later years of their careers, receive training as referees. There have been so many initiatives to keep players involved in the game, such as the 'Football in the Community' programme. Increasing numbers of ex-players are finding worthwhile employment by staying in football, but not directly as managers or coaches. Encouraging them to make a career in refereeing would prove attractive and advantageous for the game.

Finding, grooming and guiding the youngsters remains the most important single task. I fear nobody will take the initiative in England to launch a brave new era for our children. Sadly, too many talented people working in schools and youth football see their roles as merely a stepping stone to greater glory in a job with a higher profile. I would pose this question though . . . 'What's more important, personal prestige and position or the game?' There's only one answer and everybody connected with the Football Association, the Premier League, the Football League and the English Schools' FA, knows it. Something has to be done. The coaches I met with Alex Ferguson are in total agreement but who will take the initiative? It will have to be the football fuehrer.

Chapter 9

THE LAW MAKERS' CHRONICLE

'The gulf is growing between players and administrators.'

When UEFA, the governing body of European football, begin publicly appraising referees by the number of red and yellow cards they have brandished we all have reasons to fear for standards of discipline. The fact that these statistics were used to brand English referees as too lenient and explain why our officials had been overlooked for the European Championships in Sweden simply emphasised how misguided the authorities can be.

I have no doubts that our best referees are as good, if not better, than any of their fellow officials in the world. The saddest fact is that UEFA and FIFA, world soccer's rulers, are threatening the welfare of the sport they should be protecting by their policy of issuing directives to referees that effectively prevent the good officials from displaying their empathy with the competitors in a match.

I do not believe football needs to look at comprehensively re-writing the rule book. Every offence is listed within it and the referees should be left to get on with the job. Unfortunately, FIFA and UEFA are the epitome of those overblown organisations, packed with sub-committee members, who feel they must be seen to be doing something to justify their existence. The result, quite simply, is the kind of tinkering with the laws that is, at best, unnecessary and, at worst, a complete waste of time.

As the sheer size of the governing bodies grows the bureaucratic madness we witness becomes even more disturbing. Just look at the new ruling they introduced in the summer of 1992 to restrict back-passes to the goalkeeper. Back passes will be allowed, providing the 'keeper does not pick the ball up in his hands and distributes it with his feet. The motive, on the part of the law-makers, is to reduce time-wasting when the ball is in the goalie's hands or being repeatedly passed back to him by defenders. If the new rule is the authorities' idea of how to foster better football then the experiment will prove counter-productive.

Clearly, the supposition that time-wasting is not in the best interests of the game is valid. The simple solution to that would be to stamp out the one back pass that does reek of gamesmanship, the case when a goalie throws possession to a defender whose sole intention is to dally and then roll the ball back to his 'keeper. This is the most blatant and common form of time-wasting involving a back pass. As such, FIFA should have isolated it and introduced ways of dealing with this specific problem. Broadening the legal net to include all back passes is folly.

Some of the finest defenders in world football can get their teams out of a tight situation and round off their brilliant recovery work with a clever pass to their 'keeper. I still see nothing wrong with allowing a player that option. But the ruling that a goalie cannot then pick up the ball will lead to the kind of blockers and markers we've grown accustomed to in American grid iron being introduced to soccer.

UEFA used the 1991 European Youth Championships in Portugal as the test bed for the new back pass rules. I watched that competition and the masterplan was clearly ineffective. I fear that instead of improving the game and forcing defenders to turn with the ball, FIFA have inadvertently encouraged more long-ball football where teams gain an even greater advantage by pumping passes behind the opposition defence.

The new ruling will be manna from heaven to a coach working with his long-ball side. He will encourage his players not to pass to people but to deliver the ball into the space behind the markers and in front of the goalie. In the past the retreating defender would roll the ball back to his keeper but he may not be able to do that now. The clever coach will have deputed a goalie blocker or marker, whose first duty when the ball is banged forward will be to cut off the last line of defence and the opportunity for the keeper to fly-kick the ball up-field.

With the goalie effectively marked all the under-pressure defender can do is kick the ball to safety in the stand and so, with one pass, the opposition will be camped in the attacking third of the field ready to take one of their long throws towards a pack of tall players in the penalty area. This isn't a mad, scientific nightmare. This is reality as stipulated by the overlords of the world game. There's no surprise then that so many people involved in professional football believe a gulf is growing between them and the players on one side and the administrators in their ivory tower on the other.

It isn't the referees' fault. All they can do is make sure the new, unwanted laws are adhered to. But the opportunities for good referees to develop relationships with players are being diminished. The moral rights and opportunities for referees to offer protection are being wiped away.

I'll provide an insight now into why managers become so frustrated by the law-makers. A few years ago a delegate representing the Football Association flew out to a FIFA meeting in Switzerland at which the latest proposals on law amendments were to be discussed. The delegate admitted that until he sat down on the plane he had no idea what rule changes were to be discussed and, even more importantly, whether he should support the official line from head-quarters. The implications for the game were beyond him but he was told *en route* which way he should cast his vote. He claimed that was exactly what he did.

We've already lived through the syndrome of players being sent off because, as the last man in defence, they were adjudged to have fouled an attacker. If the initiative on this law was to rid the game of the cynical hack or rugby tackle nobody would support it more vehemently than me. But when the administrators insisted the law encompassed every player guilty of a foul in such a difficult to decide area of the field a gun was being placed to the referees' heads. I believed then, and still do, that the referee should have been asked to judge the intent of the defender. The rule-makers disagreed with that. The law was mandatory.

Hence, the scenario in which an experienced FIFA official like George Courtney was publicly vilified for failing to send off Leeds defender John McClelland in the FA Cup third round replay at Elland Road. George explained afterwards that, in his opinion, the defender was making a genuine attempt to win the ball and that a free-kick for Barnsley and caution for McClelland were sufficient punishment. Morally, the referee was right. He didn't have the benefit of action replays but the video recording showed that Barnsley striker Andy Rammell actually clipped his own ankles as the pair sprinted and inadvertently brought himself down.

I felt sorry for the referee in the ensuing public debate. He was in a no-win situation once the FA had pointed out that if there was a foul McClelland should have been dismissed, and in his next, high-profile, television match George duly produced a red card for Southampton's Jimmy Case. Case was some 40 yards from his own goal when he had attempted a slide tackle on Bryan Robson that the Manchester United skipper evaded. I know Robson was as stunned as Case at the sending-off but the directive had to be followed – even if both teams, both managers and match officials must have wondered if the events at Old Trafford that night in any way helped football.

There was also the classic dismissal of Blackburn Rovers' veteran defender Kevin Moran in a cup-tie against Liverpool. Ian Rush flicked the ball past Moran and the square Rovers defence, perhaps ten yards inside the opposition half, and set off. But Moran was already committed to his challenge and inevitably the pair collided.

The foul was not malicious. Moran could not have known as he went to win possession that Rush's quick-thinking would split the home defence. In fact, the only way Moran could have avoided Rush would have been if he'd taken a spade out on to the pitch to hastily dig a trench he could lie in as Rush ran over him. Rush's protests as Moran was dismissed were totally genuine. How could the rule-makers relate this kind of challenge to the appalling rugby tackles and hatchet jobs that had become commonplace when committed by despairing defenders in Spain and Italy?

The crux of the matter is that if the laws are unfair and unjust the command of the referee is lost and bad laws produce situations of genuine dispute. It dismays me that this is now a general trend in football. For years I have campaigned whenever I have been asked to speak at referee society meetings that our match officials should differentiate between the laws that truly affect the game as a spectacle and those that are related to their level of control.

Surely, the single most important factor to judge a referee by is his ability to control the match. Unfortunately, these days we're seeing some officials place greater score on punishing dissent, bad language and secondary matters like goalkeepers' steps, than the serious foul play that creates flare-ups. Football is a physical game. Heading the ball in a crowded penalty area with players crashing into one another is a potentially violent experience. Tackling an opponent fairly can involve both bravery and physical contact. Real football people can differentiate between physical contact that is an inherent part of the game, and the excessive use of violence.

When you've worked in professional football you realise the price to be paid for the unwanted excesses. I well remember during my days at Sheffield Wednesday a talented young defender called Ian Knight being felled by a wild, high tackle from Chester striker Gary Bennett in an FA Cup replay. Before that act Knight's football future looked assured. He had established himself as a calm, skilful centre-back at club level who was winning regular call-ups to the England Under-21 squad.

I can still picture the incident, in front of the main stand at Hillsborough, and while I have been accused in some quarters of being the ultimate diplomat in my post-match Press conferences I must admit that on this occasion my tolerance level had worn excruciatingly thin. Ian Knight's leg had been shattered by a tackle that surely nobody could honestly justify.

Despite his immense bravery in overcoming the catalogue of fractures to his right leg and attempting to make a comeback, Ian was understandably never the same player again. He would have been a player of genuine First Division quality. He might even have been an international-class defender. That kind of promise for the future was snatched away from him. After leaving Hillsborough he tried to rebuild his career with Grimsby but was released by them in the summer of 1991.

The spin-off from this kind of incident is inevitably a revenge motive. I know of ex-Wednesday players who moved into the lower Leagues and came across Gary Bennett and mentioned their contempt for what had happened. That is the negative side-effect of violence. You can observe it when you drive your car, when children play in the park and on the football field.

The game deteriorates when referees think foul and abusive language, often uttered within the frustration of a mistake, is a more serious offence than the kind of serious foul play that could end a player's career. We all know it's easier for a limited official to hear a player swear than spot the nasty, vengeful tackle. But it's important the good referees set the right tone in this respect.

Bad language on a football field is a moot subject. I know of one player who, after being hit twice from behind by an opponent, asked the referee to get a grip on the miscreant – and used a couple of expletives amid his painful request. Even though the striker had not retaliated and had only sought protection the ref sent him off for foul and abusive language. This particular referee might have the lowest swearing threshold in the League but this incident did happen to bring into question when 'industrial language' is permitted on the field. Certainly, in the workshop I'm sure if a joiner bangs the hammer on his finger nobody would object if he let out an oath amid his scream of pain. It's better doing that than throwing the hammer through the workshop window.

I would go further in the football context and suggest there are times when expletives can prevent a nasty situation from escalating out of hand. A frank exchange of views is better than sullen faces awaiting the major explosion when the players next meet.

I was reported to the FA during Leeds' Championship season for allegedly making foul and abusive comments to a linesman during our 6-1 victory at Sheffield Wednesday. I was delighted to eventually clear my name and create football history in two distinct fields. I became the first man to prove his innocence at a Disciplinary Commission investigating a disrepute charge and the three-man committee hearing my case allowed me to use video evidence as a crucial part of my defence.

We were winning 2-0 when the kind of incident occurred that can sour the whole competitive atmosphere of a game. Gordon Watson, the Wednesday striker, being pursued by Chris Whyte, took a dive in the penalty area to win a penalty. The Leeds players, in particular Whyte, were incensed by his actions. The fact that the game was being shown live on tele-vision meant that the player's theatrical behaviour was immediately exposed.

I was watching the game from the trainers' dug-out and ITV interviewer Gary Newbon was standing nearby with a small monitor screen. He let me see the slow-motion replays of the penalty award which confirmed my initial suspicions. I was even more concerned, though, by the anger evident among some of my team. From sailing happily towards a fine away win in a tough Yorkshire derby an act of cheating had opened up the game. Thankfully, we regained our two-goal superiority a few minutes later.

John Lukic threw possession out from goal to left-back Tony Dorigo who, without controlling the ball, sent a superb pass down the flank to Gary Speed. Speed had one touch to take the ball into his stride, then delivered a pinpoint cross that was magnificently headed home by Lee Chapman. It must have ranked as one of the best goals of the season given the precision, pace and flair of the strike. I jumped out of the dug-out to celebrate and shouted to Dorigo, the player closest to me, that he must tell Whyte to calm down. I did swear and my message was that Whyte must not get involved with 'the cheat'. The linesman patrolling the touchline in front of me flagged to the referee and I was duly cautioned. Apparently, the linesman believed I was abusing him.

It would be improper to make public now the evidence heard within the confines of the disciplinary hearing but video evidence was crucial to my case. I've heard the whispers since that I was the benefactor of an FA cover-up, that certain people in authority didn't want to see me punished. Those suggestions are ridiculous. I actually received a message from a leading FA official telling me I was wasting my time asking for a personal hearing and that I had no chance of getting off.

I took the League Managers' Association solicitor Mike Morrison to the hearing and we did notice before the commission began that there was a television and video recorder outside. We toyed with and then rejected the idea of having the equipment moved in before the tribunal commenced. I did have the video of the game with me and I was delighted when Geoff Thompson, the Chairman of the commission, agreed to let the incident be shown. Quite simply, the video replay showed the linesman must have been mistaken in his recollection of events and my positioning relative to him when he heard my comments.

A principle was established, though, that I hope other innocent parties will follow. I know the FA have said in the past that if a club wishes to send in a video of a specific incident they will allow the referee to review his decision. Normally, this can only have any bearing in a case of mistaken identity. This time I was the man who had made specific comments and the video had proved my explanation was right.

Rule changes do not happen overnight. There is a long, drawn out procedure involved but I still believe there is a dangerous oversight in not having people directly employed in the professional game as part of the legislative panel. The practitioner at club football level tends to discover the changes when they are introduced to the statute book – not during the debate.

I do appreciate the difficult jobs referees have. I try to ensure my players understand that and do not cause undue and unnecessary problems. The biggest problems for our men in black and green and purple are the directives from FIFA headquarters and the sooner the commonsense tablet is swallowed there the better.

Chapter 10

DIGGING THE DIRT

'All you can do is deal with consequences either by putting the record straight or by taking legal action.'

Behind every silver lining lurks a dark cloud and the weekend after Leeds had won the League Championship the storm clouds quickly built up on my personal horizon. The reason for my consternation was an attempt by a Sunday newspaper to create an article on the Bluebeard, evil-doing behaviour of the newly crowned Champions' manager.

Around that time it became apparent that someone was taking a particular interest in my past private life. Initially, my son Damian mentioned that he had received a telephone call at home from a gentleman who claimed he was writing my biography. He asked Damian some fairly innocuous questions that didn't add up to much but were of a personal rather than sporting nature. I also had reason to speak to an old friend from Sheffield called Pat Hanwell, whom I had played football with as a young amateur for Hallam in the Yorkshire League. Pat was trying to arrange for me to appear at a trophy presentation and, at the end of our conversation, he mentioned as a rider that the biography shortly to be published should make interesting reading because he had been approached by a mysterious gentleman who had also been tracking down my old schoolmates and former colleagues.

By this stage I was becoming increasingly suspicious of the whole matter because no publisher or writer had made an approach to me and the questions he directed to the people concerned also seemed a little strange. The volcano was rumbling and the explosion seemed imminent when I received a call from my ex-wife Lynne. She was agitated, to put it mildly, because she had received two very unsettling 'phone calls.

The first, that morning, had come from a lady purporting to work for the Government's National Insurance office. She claimed, as a result of losing records, they were keen to verify certain facts. She wanted to check Lynne's maiden name, her old address and whether she had been married to a certain Howard Wilkinson. Fortunately, Lynne had the presence of mind to ask where the inquirer was calling from, and when told London, pointed out that all National Insurance matters for her area were dealt with from Newcastle. Unless the lady had concrete evidence to prove her enquiries were *bone fide* Lynne did not want to continue the conversation.

Soon afterwards, Lynne received another call, this time from a gentleman who came clean and admitted he was a freelance journalist working on behalf of a national newspaper and investigating claims that there were unsavoury circumstances surrounding our eventual divorce. He seemed to think these rumours were of national importance and worthy of tabling before the great British public.

To her immense credit, Lynne told the man, quite bluntly, where to go and put him right about the so-called story he had suggested to her. He was not easily dissuaded though because during the conversation he suggested she could make a lot of money from such an exposé if only she would co-operate. Lynne found the journalist's views and professional approach abhorrent and told him so in no uncertain terms.

Predictably, by this stage, there were many people in my family circle becoming very upset at the prospect of a story being splashed in a Sunday newspaper, particularly as the story had no basis in fact.

During the course of the day I set about trying to trace the source of all the trouble and with the help of two friends who are journalists – ordinary, decent men – we managed to find the gentleman concerned and the newspaper, in vague terms, he represented. He wasn't a staff man working for any national title. He was a freelance reporter who dug up his stories and then found a market. For my part, because of my experience and a degree of cynicism, I wasn't surprised or too upset. I had come to realise that if certain sections of the media want to run a story they'll go ahead and do it. There's little or nothing you can do or say that will halt them in their tracks.

All you can do is deal with the consequences either by putting the record straight or by taking legal action. That appears to be one of the penalties of being in a high-profile job and having achieved a little success. The intention was to run the story at an opportune time – probably the day after the FA Cup final between Liverpool and Sunderland.

The journalist concerned found no evidence to base his story on and was forced to accept this, given the response of my first wife and other close friends. As such the investigation was stopped. The photographs of our extended family celebrations when the Championship had been won did a little to underline the lies the journalist was trying to tell. I have to congratulate him, though, for his persistence and do believe he tried something similar a few years earlier when I was at Sheffield Wednesday. On that occasion his seed again fell on stony ground. He found nothing to his benefit that he could use against me.

I also have to congratulate him for his tenacity in tracking down so many long-lost relatives Lynne had not spoken to for years. Suddenly, they were all coming forward with tales of mysterious calls from a journalist investigating our marital breakdown. I must admit there was a mischievous notion in my mind when I meditated on the topics of justice and fair play about the prospect of a sizeable libel settlement if the story had been run. But, overall, while I might personally have relished a court case the best outcome for my family was for us collectively to know the truth and for the journalist to curtail his enquiries.

Unfortunately, it is a fact of life that football personalities play an increasingly prolific part in the news editorial side of newspapers rather than just the sports pages. Players and people involved in the game, because of their massive earning potential, are assumed to be in the public eye and legitimate targets for certain types of tacky journalism. It's a very difficult situation and when you've been involved as long as I have you do tend to become cynical and find it hard to resist the feeling that only a minority of what actually appears in certain of our newspapers is based on truth.

Satisfying the public's supposed craving for intimate details of private lives means that newspapers tread a fine line. On the positive side I can cite in recent months the respect for privacy afforded Gary and Michelle Lineker when their baby George was so tragically diagnosed as suffering from leukaemia. I know the Linekers appreciated the lack of intrusion and were well aware of the support of the nation in their time of family crisis. Yet, we also had the treatment meted out to Prince Charles and Princess Diana when intimate details of their lives were publicised and then debated. I felt many newspapers did degenerate to the level of salacious voyeurs when covering the problems in the private Royal marriage.

It would be wrong to suggest this unsavoury phenomenon only happens in Britain – it doesn't. I had to smile when Paul Gascoigne suggested the opportunity to escape the British media was of paramount importance behind his transfer to Lazio of Rome. The slightest indiscretion in Italy will be seized upon by a Press ready to publicly vilify any highly paid star who fails to behave impeccably.

I'm sure Eric Cantona will also support that view if you believe everything he and his associates tell you about his treatment at the hands of the media in France. Eric created a massive amount of publicity in France as he developed an unwanted reputation as 'Le Brat' – a reputation which has not been evident in any way during his time with Leeds.

They say in showbusiness, 'No publicity is bad publicity' and in Eric's case the Press coverage he has received in England has worked largely to his advantage. Whether the price Eric, or anyone else, has to pay is worthwhile, I have my doubts. In my own case, I would be happy to be left alone to get on with my job – but that is not going to happen.

Eric's arrival at Elland Road was heralded by unprecedented media attention, much of it from France. On the day he made his debut at Oldham he literally would not leave the dressing-room before the game because of the number of cameramen and reporters crammed into the players' tunnel at Boundary Park. Eric had to win over the media in this country as well as the fans.

In that respect, I think he has proved the most successful acquisition Leeds have ever made. Even with the obvious language difficulties he has presented a refreshing new angle on Leeds United affairs. If you rated his popularity with the fans against the hours and minutes he has been out on that pitch he must be the greatest hero the Leeds supporters have ever had. All of which is hard to comprehend but that's the entertainment side of football which we know exists. You can't analyse it too comprehensively without scratching your head at its irrationality. Put simply, as far as the public are concerned, Eric clearly has star quality.

As far as I'm concerned I hope my faith in his ability is justified and he produces star quality on the field because without that he has nothing and I have even less. Signing Eric was a gamble but after just two or three days in training I knew we were witnessing a player of special natural talents. The big question now is whether he has the character and intelligence to adapt that ability. We still don't know but, in that respect, the next season or so will be make-or-break for Eric.

Realistically, if you scrutinise the evidence you have to admit his chances are less than even. While English players have largely done well abroad the success of foreign imports to England has not been as marked. Perhaps most critical of all is Eric's playing position as a striker. I can't think of any genuine forward who has come from abroad and been a long-term success here. It has been the players in other departments – like midfielders Ossie Ardiles, Arnold Muhren and Franz Thijssen – who have illuminated our game over a matter of years.

The reason for that is the fundamental problem of playing styles – especially for strikers. The Europeans – outside these shores – have developed their approach to the game. That style varies slightly from south and eastern Europe to north and west but, basically, there's a way of playing that involves a form of man-to-man marking, employs a sweeper and plays in a way that allows defending to be concentrated in your own half. The team without possession will happily concede ground and wait for the opportunity to pounce.

Therefore, in the early stages of an attacking build-up there is a degree of composed possession and a degree of time and space that does not exist in this country. Here the tendency is for defending to commence once possession is lost. Wherever you are on the pitch you have far less room and space than 90 per cent of Europe's football population. If you agree with me that style tends to produce type then obviously the football that succeeds in this country is different to that which succeeds on the continent. Tempo is a much used word and with its implied reference to dance and music it does create a fitting analogy. The tempo here is much quicker. In dancing terms we rock-and-roll while the rest of Europe waltzes.

There is a problem, though, in that the style we adopt

produces characteristics. Unfortunately, in football's world theatre the nuances acquired in England can appear to have less relevance and be less effective, particularly when watered down in a mistaken effort to move towards a continental type of game.

The England manager tends to be good when we win while the roof falls in after an international defeat, so winning is what's important. I feel we're probably better looking at what we do best and trying to do it even better at the top level. If you look at the situation in a deeper, more aesthetic way you can head in a totally different direction. If we altered the principles of play at our clubs I'm sure we could eventually produce footballers who are capable of winning more and winning in a more pleasing way. Some of my rival managers may dispute that statement.

The crux of the problem, though, is bringing that kind of change of attitude into English football. I'm well aware that many sports writers keep repeating that that is the avenue we should now be heading down but achieving that goal is so difficult because style is not just a product of what you set out to do, it's a product of how opponents allow you to play. The dilemma revolves around getting players to be composed and comfortable in all situations when they don't get the chance to practise those skills in English match situations. The game in England has developed with a guiding principle at its core, that opponents will not allow you time and space.

If we were to successfully pursue a change in doctrine we would probably need football to be taken over by a dictator who, at a stroke, would decide that every team above a certain level would play in a certain way. I'm well aware there are those English teams who have traditionally attempted, and continue to try, to pass the ball in all areas of the pitch. Ultimately, they tend not to be successful, not the teams that win League Championships. They do give pleasure at times but their unpredictability is actually predictable because measures can be taken to deal with the passing teams if they don't have the best individual players in the country.

In my opinion that was Liverpool's greatest strength when they were omnipotent in the League, and I stress League because that was the acid test always cited as crucial within the Anfield bootroom. The Liverpool style was not only a product of the way the game should be played but related to the quality of the players involved and their individual capability to impress the Liverpool approach on opponents no matter what the opposition threw at them.

This returns us to the Catch 22 questions for Catona. Can Eric adapt to life in England or can we adapt to Cantona? Do I ask him to change or do I ask Leeds to change to the French style? In the long days of summer sunshine with time for theoretical debates about the game and the battles to be fought on the distant horizon you may reach some edifying conclusions. Experience tells me that in the mid-winter slog, when the helter-skelter of Premier League football starts to bite and we have all donned our tin hats, the most fundamental word that will spring to mind is . . . 'survival'.

Providing Cantona with the stage on which he can grace us with his skills is one thing. We must attempt to embrace his talent within our British approach and grow together. There will be no French revolution because that, in our football terms, would inevitably suffer a defeat. But Eric can make our players better just as they can help him. The type of football and invention they produce can be brighter and much more attractive by a united effort. We just have to make sure our collective efforts remain the best.

POSTSCRIPT

I believe it's absolutely crucial to surround yourself with good, common-sense, down-to-earth people. Just as children grow and benefit from the positive influences of reasonable and caring parents in attendance most of the time, for a manager, good staff can have a very similar effect.

I remember well, a few days after I'd moved into the job at Sheffield Wednesday, taking my son Damian for a tour around the imposing and impressive stadium. Surprisingly, Damian, then only 12 years old, couldn't hide his impatience as we toured the gym, the weight room, trod the hallowed turf, opened the doors on the magical boot room. Finally, his secret wish got the better of him. 'Dad, when can I see your office?' I grew by the second, pumped up by a parent's pride. Not for my son the trappings and trivia, he wanted to see where his dad would sweat and toil, he wanted the see the reality of a manager's existence.

I took him inside the office which was only slightly more impressive than the room I'd occupied at homely Notts County. I started to explain what the charts meant, but before I could get more than a couple of words out he was behind the desk and ensconced in the manager's chair. He sat there as if he'd been born to the job, hands splayed and resting confidently on the arms of the chair, shoulders back, head held high and legs outstretched in a pose which told newcomers to the room that the desk and all present are part and parcel of the incumbent's kingdom.

It was one of those poignant moments so very dear to every father. He pushed his feet against the desk and swivelled the chair. It rotated slowly; he was totally in control. 'Wait until I go to school on Monday and tell my mates . . . I sat in Jack Charlton's chair!'

I swear you could hear the thud as my feet hit the ground, the whoosh of out-rushing air as my balloon burst. There's little danger of flying at altitude with people like that around you, and as far as I'm concerned, the more, the merrier!